Good Loving

Good Loving

How Christian Couples Can Discover Sexual Intimacy, Pleasure and Fulfillment

Melissa Jones, PhD

Ulysses Press

Published in the United States by
Ulysses Press
P.O. Box 3440
Berkeley, CA 94703
www.ulyssespress.com

ISBN: 978-1-61243-396-7
Library of Congress Control Number 2014943023

Printed in Canada by Marquis Book Printing

10 9 8 7 6 5 4 3 2 1

Acquisitions Editor: Katherine Furman
Managing Editor: Claire Chun
Editors: Erin Collins, Christian Heftel
Copyeditor: Renee Rutledge
Proofreader: Lauren Harrison
Layout: Lindsay Tamura
Index: Sayre Van Young
Front cover design: Robin Artz
Cover photograph: © EpicStockMedia/shutterstock.com
Interior design: what!design @ whatweb.com
Illustrations on pages 116 and 127 by Rick Williamson

IMPORTANT NOTE TO READERS: This book is independently authored and published and no sponsorship or endorsement of this book by, and no affiliation with, any trademarked brands or other products mentioned within is claimed or suggested. All trademarks that appear in this book belong to their respective owners and are used here for informational purposes only. The authors and publishers encourage readers to patronize the quality brands mentioned in this book.

Contents

Preface

I am a wife, a mother, and a woman of faith. And I am a sexologist. I help people who want to improve their sex lives, increase their intimacy, and experience more pleasure. I speak at conferences and conduct workshops where I talk about G-zone stimulation, multiple male orgasms, oral sex, and a variety of other topics regarding intimacy between couples.

I've often been asked how I reconcile both parts of my life: my conservative beliefs and my work. Some may think that because I'm Christian, I can't believe in anything but vanilla, missionary-position, lights-off sex. Some seem to think that giving and receiving pleasure, even in a loving and committed marriage, must be some sort of offense toward God.

Not only do I see no conflict between having good sex and being a good Christian, but I firmly believe that they actually support each other. I believe that marriage and sex were created by God, and I believe that we are designed to take pleasure in both.

Although this book can be read by anyone, my intended audience is traditional, married couples that hope to improve their sex lives and strengthen their relationships. This book can also be used by soon-to-be-married couples that hope to prevent sexual issues before they start (although complete novices may have a few eye-widening moments if they read this book from cover to cover). It's not my intention to be salacious or obscene, but I am explicit so as to avoid confusion, and I don't beat around the bush. I believe that sex is something to be celebrated, not to be ashamed of, and I would rather err on the side of giving you too much information than too little.

Either partner can read this book and benefit from it; however, you will experience the greatest benefit if you both discuss and do the exercises together. Sex is a dance that works best when two partners move in sync with each other and grow together. In this way, you will grow closer and bring each other more pleasure and happiness than you may have thought possible.

I also have a number of exercises that I encourage you to try. Some will be more exciting and productive than others, and there may be some exercises that you don't want to do at all. Each was designed to assist with a specific aspect of one's sex life. If you get stuck or find that an exercise isn't working for you, skip it and move on.

The first section in this book will address foundational issues of sex in marriage. Part Two is an escalation of couple's exercises. It's ideal to read these in the order presented here, rather than simply jumping to the exercises.

Each couple's situation is different. For some, this book may be too much; for others, you may need more. (In that case, call me.) We all make decisions about what we think is appropriate sexually, and even though we may have similar cultural values, we may not place our sexual boundaries in exactly the same place. My intent is neither to push you beyond your values nor to limit you to mine. My goal is to make you aware of some of the possibilities that are out there so that you can make informed decisions as a couple. As you do this, you will develop greater emotional closeness and sexual vibrancy.

Although my practice is based in San Antonio, Texas, I perform consultations for clients all over the world via telephone and video chat, so if you need a little extra help, I invite you to visit with me. For more information, please visit my website at www.MelissaJonesPhD.com.

I suggest that you regard this book—and sex in general—like a grand buffet in a beautiful hall with hundreds of dishes, ranging from foie gras and caviar to chicken fried steak with gravy. You may not love every dish you taste, but there's a good chance that if you are willing to try something new, you'll discover something quite savory!

Bon appétit!

Part I

This section is directed toward you as an individual and the possible issues you may be facing, as well as those your spouse may be experiencing. I won't discuss every potential issue—the list would be too long—and I won't offer a solution to every problem discussed. This section is to acknowledge the potential issues; solutions will come as you work on the exercises found in this section as a couple, and seek additional help where needed.

Chapter 1

Intimacy

A number of years ago, I was a camp leader for the young women in my church. One night, when all of the girls had gone to bed, the adult counselors—all practicing Christian women—stayed up talking. This night, the talk turned to sex. I was surprised and dismayed to hear that many of these wonderful women just weren't happy with their sex lives. Some of them seemed to think that sex was only meant for procreation. Others thought that its only purpose was to make their husbands happy. Some of the women had been married for years, or even decades, and had never experienced an orgasm.

A number of these women were just "getting by" sexually, and many of them were really struggling. Some of them had marriages affected by infidelity and pornography, and some were on the verge of breakup. It saddened me to hear about the women whose marriages were in danger. But it also saddened me to hear about the women who simply weren't enjoying sex.

Marriages should be havens of intimacy, but how do we attain it? Part of the confusion results from our imprecision in defining "intimacy." Some people use it to mean a general feeling of emotional closeness. Some define it as friendship. And others simply use it as a word that's synonymous with "sex," but is simply more appropriate to say in church.

In reality, intimacy has a myriad of aspects. It derives from the Latin word *intimus*, which means "innermost," or "the deepest within." The people with whom we are intimate are the people that we let in and the people who let us in in return.

There are different kinds of intimacy in marriage: intellectual, emotional, spiritual, etc. Equally important, though, is physical, erotic intimacy. The intimacies in our relationships build on each other like instruments in a symphony, each providing counterpoint and context for the others, each contributing to the overall vibrancy of the marriage.

Working with religious couples, I get to see marriages where the spouses are deeply committed and have closeness from building a family and working together on goals. However, many of these couples confess that the spark is missing from their relationship. Some of the romance is gone, and they feel more like platonic friends, amicable roommates, or even brothers and sisters than like lovers.

Although they have some types of intimacy, these couples may be missing sexual intimacy. And while some seem perfectly fine without romance, I know that neglecting sex can severely weaken a marriage. No matter how strong you consider your marriage to be, if you enhance your sexual intimacy, your relationship will be stronger and better able to weather the difficulties that couples inevitably encounter.

Just as spices can give zest to food, good sex can make marital relationships come alive.

Couples may not always consciously realize that they crave sexual intimacy. Couples who wish that they could return to their courting days or to their time as newlyweds are often unconsciously expressing an urge to return to a time of sexual desire for each other. Although it's impossible to turn back the clock, the couple can build sexual desire and intimacy now. Even more than that, it's possible to make your sex life much better than it was in your early days!

According to my understanding of the scriptures, sexual intimacy is not merely a good idea; it's a commandment (albeit a very fun one). In Proverbs, we read, "Rejoice with the wife of thy youth ... Let her breasts satisfy thee at all times, and be thou ravished always with her love."[1] And in Genesis, we read that "a man shall leave his father and his mother and shall cleave unto his wife, and the two shall be one flesh."[2]

We're never closer to being one flesh than when we are sexually intimate. When we're in the middle of having good sex, we feel joyfully, ecstatically close to our partners. And it bears fruit outside of the bedroom as well: good sex puts a smile on our faces when we see our partners, a lift in our steps when we anticipate coming home, and a sparkle in our eyes whenever we think about them.

Every couple I meet is unique, but some are more special than others and stick in my memory. Tom and Claire were one such couple. (All names have been changed and permission has been granted to relate their stories.)

1　Proverbs 5:18-19
2　Genesis 2:24

When a couple enters my office, I make it a point to notice which of them enters first. I try to read their body language to determine if he is leading her to the session or if he is ushering her in, and it's just as often the woman doing the leading or the pushing.

On this Thursday afternoon, Tom walked into my office for the first time. His eyes went quickly from me to the floor. He was taller and more muscular than his photo had indicated, and he was better dressed than most men are at 2 p.m.—obviously an alpha male, but this wasn't his den and he wasn't in charge. Following him was Claire. She was polite and less than half his size, but very much running the show at the moment. She held my gaze and shook my hand firmly.

Their intake paperwork (obviously written by her) told me why they were here. I'd read it when they booked the appointment a week before, and again just after my previous client had left, yet I still wanted to have them tell me what had brought them in. Before asking them, I started by reading their interpersonal body language. My interview room is large; the back half has the traditional therapist setup: my armless brown leather chair facing a settee fit for two. The front half of the office has a huge, L-shaped, red leather couch.

I made a wide gesture to the whole room as I said to them, "Have a seat." Before they could ask where, I turned my back and offered them something to drink—"Water? Coke?" —while I walked to my fridge. Most couples take the settee, but a few take the red couch because it lets them sit as far apart from each other as possible, and on those occasions I've sometimes actually sat between them—either to pull them in both close to me and to each other, or to act as referee. On this day, Tom opted for the couch, where he flopped down on his side and curled up, and she sat by his head, stroking his hair as he covered his eyes with his hands, trying to hold in tears. And so began our first session.

There are a number of reasons why couples struggle with sexual intimacy. I mentioned earlier that the various types of intimacies build on each other. Couples who struggle with their sexual intimacy sometimes do so because other areas in their relationship are lagging. It's hard to look forward to being intimate with someone if you don't respect them or if you think they don't respect you. Likewise, if you are fuming because you just had a huge fight, you probably aren't looking forward to having sex with them.

For those struggling to understand one another, I often encourage couples to discover their love languages.[3] Couples with even more serious issues may benefit from traditional marriage therapy. Clearing up relationship issues helps lay a foundation upon which one can build sexual intimacy.

Some may struggle with intimacy because of past trauma, such as sexual abuse. Such problems are largely beyond the scope of this book. Although those who have suffered so may find some of the exercises worthwhile, it may be best to work through these issues with the help of professional counseling.

As covered within the scope of this book, there are a number of reasons why couples struggle with intimacy, such as simply not prioritizing sex. In their busy, hurried lives, they do not take enough time to just play together and make love. Others lack sexual intimacy because they lack sexual

---

3 See *The Five Love Languages*, by Gary Chapman.

skills. Making love is an art form, like playing a musical instrument, painting, or dancing. It takes time and practice to learn how to enjoy your partner's body.

Challenges to Intimacy

Just as different people have different turn-ons, the *degree* of sexual desire a person has can also vary greatly. Because of this, it's very rare that a couple never experiences differences in sexual desire, and it's perfectly fine to acknowledge this. Denying these differences can lead to frustration, tension, and resentment. However, understanding and communication can help to bridge differences in sexual desire and allow both partners to find satisfaction.

If your spouse is less interested in sex than you are, it's easy to wonder, "Does she still find me attractive?" or "Did I do something to make him upset?" In reality, it's probably something different entirely, but unless it's addressed, you just assume the worst. Even if you find out that your spouse is less interested in sex because of something that you've done (or haven't done), then knowing about it lets you work toward regaining intimacy.

Finally, communication can help bridge the gap between the partners' desire levels by making room for sexual compromises. If a man really wants to have sex with his wife, but she's too tired or preoccupied to feel like she can let go and really enjoy it, she may still feel up to kissing. Solutions like this can help maintain intimacy, even when the situation makes for a difference in desire levels.

The libido is a complicated thing with simple wishes, but it can be affected by a variety of factors. I'm going to mention a few here by way of acknowledging that you're not alone. To detail all the possible problems would be an endless list, and our purpose isn't to "pathologize" a person's lack of intimacy, but rather to admit that it exists and then provide the means via the exercises in this book to overcome it.

As you consider why intimacy may be lacking in your relationship, consider whether the relationship is lacking arousal, physical stimulation, a physical response to stimulation, emotional satisfaction, etc. Try to break down sex into its components and see if you can pinpoint what you're lacking. Pinpointing the problem won't necessarily help you solve it at this time, but as you join in the exercises, you'll have this in the back of your mind and be able to work toward a solution together.

Obstacles to Sexual Intimacy

The potential obstacles in a sexual relationship are endless, so I will touch briefly on a few of the more common ones. That's right, I said common. Facing these types of obstacles in your relationship is far from unheard of, and by making yourself aware of them, you better prepare yourself to take steps toward conquering them.

Environmental distractions—from work and children to video games and pornography—can detract from your sex life if you let them. There can also be serious psychological factors at play, such as a crisis of identity or mood, or one partner's past traumatic experience. Some partners even play psychological games with one another, using sex as a weapon or tool. This has disastrous effects, not only on your sexual relationship, but on your marriage as a whole.

Mother Nature herself can also tamper with your sex life. A simple illness or a lack of sleep may cause you to lose interest in sex temporarily. Hormonal imbalances can also affect your libido, but modern medicine has many options for handling low estrogen or testosterone, so speak to a doctor if you feel this may be an issue.

There are some medications that can have a negative effect on your libido—birth control, antidepressants, and blood pressure medications, just to name a few. Discuss the trade-offs and possible alternatives with your doctor if you feel this is a concern. There may be another type of medication to treat your condition that won't affect your sex life.

Your libido (or your partner's libido) can also be influenced simply by the stage of life you're in. This is especially true in women. Pregnancy, childbirth, and caring for a newborn child all have effects on a woman's sex drive. Later in life, menopause can also affect a woman's hormones and even the physical appearance of her body, including her genitals, which can seriously affect your sexual relationship.

As exhaustive as this list may seem, there are countless, more subtle, reasons why sexual intimacy can suffer. The good news is that intimacy *can* be achieved. Rest assured that you can get the spark back and regain the desire that you once felt for each other.

Revealing Exercise

Do this little thought exercise by yourself. Imagine that you ask your spouse to join you for a conversation regarding sexual interests. You two are sitting alone at the table or on the couch and are thinking of your most intimate sexual desire—that sexual yearning you crave more than any other.

Now imagine your spouse's reaction. How does he/she look? Are you picturing him/her as shocked, appalled, horrified, or angry? Or do you think he/she will say, "Thank you so much for telling me..."?

Which of these scenarios is more likely? Even if the second option is possible, the smallest fear of rejection may halt you from fully disclosing. But wouldn't it be so satisfying and wonderful if you could have this kind of discussion? Alternatively, would you be willing to have your spouse tell you their most personal desires and interests even if they don't match yours? How well could you tolerate discovering that your spouse has a sexual interest that you didn't know about? It's not uncommon to be anxious about disclosing a secret desire to a spouse, especially one that may not be reciprocated, but true love means loving each other despite the differences.

Chapter 2

"What's Okay?"

When clients' emotions run deep, I often slow things down to give them time to disclose at their own pace, but such was not the case with Tom. As he lay on my couch, he just started blubbering about all the "sexual sins" he'd committed and how he was ruining their marriage. Oddly, for being a dishonored wife, Claire just rolled her eyes and shrugged her shoulders in indifference.

As Tom told me more and more about what he'd done, I quickly learned that Claire wasn't bothered by his "transgressions" as much as she was doubtful that he'd done anything wrong. Usually when a husband confesses to sexual improprieties, the wife is profoundly distraught, but in this case, his pent-up errors were insignificant to her, and so while awaiting an appointment with their minister, she encouraged him to come tell me his sexual troubles.

Most books on sex don't ask the question "What's okay?" I want to address this right up front so we can deal with it and move on.

People who grow up in faith-based homes receive a lot of beneficial instruction. They're often taught the importance of family, of marriage, of love. They're taught to respect their bodies through modesty and chastity before marriage. Many believe these guidelines are incredibly important, and they find peace and meaning in living these principles. They believe that these ideals help them prepare to be intimate with their future spouse.

However, along with these helpful virtues, we also receive some unhelpful messages. Well-meaning teachers who try to impress the importance of chastity on their students sometimes resort to lessons and strategies that attach fear and shame to sex. These messages may help to keep people chaste prior to marriage, but they do so at a cost. The negative emotions that these lessons attach to sex can result in intense guilt. Even more problematic, the damage can linger long after the wedding bells have rung. Left unchecked, these negative views of sex will disrupt a couple's sexual intimacy and ultimately weaken the marriage.

These feelings also take a toll on the individuals themselves. It's hard to navigate between living with guilt and questioning long-held beliefs; the passage may not be obvious, but it is possible.

There are many different beliefs regarding the propriety of sex. Some believe that the only acceptable purpose is to bear children. Others feel that sex can be used to bring couples closer together, but that it should be limited in its scope. Some feel that even if both spouses are consenting, only certain acts are permissible. The list goes on. There are about as many different interpretations of sexual morality as there are people in the pews.

Let's finish the story of Tom and Claire. The crux of Tom's declaration was that he had recently confessed to Claire, his wife of five years, that he had been unfaithful to her. (To this, she rolled her eyes again.) It took a little more prodding, but I finally got him to say it: "Unfaithful in my thoughts," he said. I silently waited for the other shoe to drop, but there was nothing more than that.

So she took over the storytelling as he hid his face from me: For the past couple of years, he had harbored a sexual fantasy that festered in his mind. Even though it made him blush as she related it, the fantasy was nothing more erotic than what 99 percent of other men have imagined, and probably what 90 percent of men have done with their wives, but to this man, this desire was a grave sin in need of purging. And this good man was racked with guilt over it. (In a later session, his wife even said that she was interested in trying it.) Here was a kind man who had the standard of morality set so high that he was destined for failure and was fully experiencing the consequences right here on my red leather couch.

Despite the title of this chapter, I'm not going to give you a list of what's acceptable and what's not—sorry to disappoint. I'm not even going to try to convince you that what I feel regarding sex is right. Each person and each couple needs to decide for themselves what their sexual boundaries are. What I'd like to do is to encourage you to think about *how* you formed your sexual boundaries. That's what I told Tom and Claire to do.

First, recognize that there could exist a difference between your *beliefs*, your *religious teachings,* and your *culture*. I use the term *beliefs* to mean those attitudes that you have been taught and now hold dear to you. Your *religious teachings* are those doctrines or messages your faith preaches to you. And your *culture* is the generally accepted attitude on how people ought to live.

Recognize that these are not all the same thing. Ideally, these three should be in harmony, but don't assume that they automatically are. Consider that it may be worthwhile to ponder if these are all in balance in your life. Many people act as if these three are all the same thing and are troubled when considering that they may not be. I would hope that your faith invites you to ponder and seek clarification.

Think back to where you received the rules regarding which sexual behaviors are and aren't acceptable. Did they come from a parent, a teacher, a minister? Did you ever wonder where *they* got them from? Will you pass those same rules on to your children "as is"? Are you passing along your own beliefs, your community's culture, or your religion's doctrines?

I've even seen instances where, in my opinion, cultural practices actually contradict the religion's central doctrines. In such cases, conscientious couples must decide which to follow and may have to tolerate some shunning.

Not long ago, I received a very heartfelt email from a woman asking me to take her on as a client. She enjoyed an active sex life in her marriage and was faithful in her conservative religion. She was seeking guidance from me on how to navigate the balance between her sexual desires and her religion's teachings. While she acknowledged that my role was not to be her conscience or spiritual guide, she concluded her request with, "I know you can't grant me permission, right?"

As a Mormon,[4] I've often been asked by fellow members if such-and-such is okay. Being asked that question gives me an opportunity to teach an important lesson. I respond, "To whom?" They look confused so I must rephrase their question: "You asked me if it's okay, so I ask, 'To whom is it okay?' If you're asking *me* if it's okay, I'll say yes. If you ask your wife if it's okay, she'll say, only when she's in the mood. If you ask your minister's wife, she'll say, 'Well, I never!' But if you want to know if it's okay to God, then you need to ask Him."

My answer is a little snarky, but it makes the point—don't seek others' approval or condemnation for things that are sacred between you and your spouse. The opinions that matter are of those in the bedroom. I won't dissuade you from seeking the opinions of others, but you will be up for a daunting challenge as you scour the texts for vague case law to both support and refute your passions. In fact, to my understanding, there is no scripture that plainly prohibits certain sexual acts or limits sexual activities within the bounds of marriage in any way.

In my experience, even after such a laborious intellectual pursuit (which is likely to turn up no real results), desires won't have been extinguished, but will continue to smolder under the weight of confusion, guilt, and avoidance. Ultimately, the fire will erupt, either in an igniting of the relationship or in a scorching of the individuals' sensuality.

---

4   The actual name of the church is The Church of Jesus Christ of Latter-day Saints.

In most Christian religions, sex is described as a good and wonderful thing within the bounds of marriage, as a way for couples to express their love and grow closer to each other and as a holy act of creation in which spouses emulate the divine. To emphasize sex's essential holiness, some have even used the word "sacrament" to describe it.

However, despite the fact that sex is understood in doctrine to be beautiful and holy, I've seen some absolutely horrendous lessons taught on the subject. One abject lesson promoting chastity involved a teacher licking the frosting off of a cupcake and then asking the class if anyone still wanted a bite. Another compared sexual sin to pounding nails into a board: even after the nails are removed, huge, ugly gashes are left in the wood. Lessons like this have taken a significant toll on some of the couples with whom I work.

Rather than seeking answers on an organizational or cultural level, I believe that the best way to decide what is appropriate in marital relations is in the context of the marriage. The question that couples should ask is, "How can my marriage become more intimate, loving, exciting, and fulfilling for myself and my partner?" Rather than stressing over where the lines of "okay" and "not okay" lie, why not be more concerned with pursuing activities that will build your marriage the way you want it built? In this view, you will know which sexual acts are acceptable "by their fruits"[5]—by what they do for your relationship. This delineation is one that I have seen help numerous marriages and is the stance that I recommend.

I've also met some shy couples who would actually welcome a short list of "allowed practices" simply because they

5 Matthew 7:20

are nervous about trying something new. Their reluctance is based on the admonition given to them: "If it makes you uncomfortable, don't do it." In my opinion, this is unhelpful (and frankly bad) advice. I sometimes find work uncomfortable, but in the end I'm very glad I did it. Many couples have sexual hang-ups that have nothing whatsoever to do with their faith, but they use their religion as a convenient shield to protect them from doing new things. (Too bad my religion won't protect me from broccoli.) Step out of your comfort zone and try something new.

In my opinion, couples should cultivate an attitude of exuberant exploration in their marriages. Instead of maintaining only a list of allowed practices, couples should expand their horizons and try to become more comfortable with different sexual options. This doesn't mean engaging in activities they find repugnant. It just means the more options you have, the more ways you have to connect with your spouse.

Finally, despite everything I've written above, it's still common for young spouses to have different opinions about what is and isn't acceptable to each of them. And given their different experiences, that's understandable. Spouses have different views in just about every area, including how toothpaste tubes should be squeezed and which way the toilet paper should hang. Why would we expect sex to be any different? The expectation is that, with time and communication, you'll come to better understand each other's sexual interests.

Sexual differences are just another place where marriage allows us the ability to expand our souls and learn to accommodate the attitudes of another person. Sharing one's sexual desires can take a lot of bravery. As much as possible, treat variances in sexual beliefs as differences in taste, not morality. If your spouse is interested in a sexual act that you find unpleasant, you aren't obligated to perform it. You should never have to do anything sexually that you are opposed to.

But just because you don't like something today doesn't mean that you can never develop a liking for it. My Grandpa Price gave the following advice to my mom, who then passed it along to me: "If you try something and you don't like it, try it again a year later." Regardless of outcome, you do need to show respect for your partner and gratitude to them for opening up.

On the other hand, if your spouse is disinterested in a sexual act that you like, don't just try to force it. Be respectful and patient. With time and communication, you will develop avenues that may be acceptable (and amazing) for both of you.

I've used the following exercise to help couples discover what their beliefs are regarding sex.

Exercise: Understanding Your Sexual Beliefs

Each of you get a notebook. Then, take some time alone to think about and write answers to each of the questions below. You may want to do this exercise in more than one sitting, as it can take time to make a thorough and honest accounting of your feelings.

1. What were my earliest instructions about sex? Who taught me? How do I think that person obtained their understanding of sexual beliefs?
2. What is my first memory of experiencing sexual feelings? Was it a positive or negative experience at the time?
3. How did my feelings regarding sex change and what may have caused them to change?
4. What lessons regarding sexuality did I receive from…
   a) My parents?
   b) My peers?
   c) My church/school?
5. What lessons did I receive regarding masturbation and how do those affect me now?
6. What guidance did I receive regarding pornography?
7. How does what I learned in my childhood affect the way I feel about sex today?
8. What lessons have I received regarding …
   a) Sexual behavior prior to marriage?
   b) Sexual behavior in marriage?
9. Of my beliefs regarding sex, which are core that I can't forsake and which are less so?
10. What are the implications of violating/forsaking a core belief?

11. With which sources of instruction must I comply and with which sources may I differ? Why?
12. How do my views of sex differ from my partner's? How well do I accept these differences?
13. Are there sexual acts to which I am not morally opposed, but avoid for other reasons?
14. Do I have any desires that conflict with my beliefs? How do I manage that conflict?
15. What role do guilt and shame play in my sexual desires and actions?
16. Do my spouse or I have unnecessary guilt? How might it be overcome?
17. What do I want to teach my children about sex, and how does this compare to what I was taught?

When you finish, share with your spouse whatever answers you feel comfortable sharing. Ideally, you would share everything on your lists. However, if something feels too personal at this point, you do have the option not to share it. Feeling compelled to share everything may make it harder for you to be honest with yourself.

As you discuss your answers with your spouse, remember to be respectful and courteous. Nothing shuts down communication faster than criticism.

Chapter 3

Guilt

One of the most common sexual issues confronting religious couples is guilt. This can lead to fear of sex itself, or fear of expressing intimate desires. Unfortunately, I see many couples that carry guilt into their relationships and quickly fall into bad habits of not communicating about their true passions. They either ignore the problem or endure sex because it's what married people do, not because they enjoy the interaction. Sadly, both partners are being let down with this approach.

Pleasure Guilt

I once had a couple visit me that had been married for almost twenty years. They loved each other dearly and had an accomplished family. However, the wife had recently admitted to her husband that she had never enjoyed sex and had actually never had an orgasm. As one may imagine, he was devastated. He was willing to do anything to make her happy. By the time they reached my office, he had read many self-help books without success.

As we talked, it became very clear that the wife grew up in a very conservative home in which sex was never discussed and her parents never showed intimacy to each other. She also heard her mother complain about sex—that it was a chore and a wifely duty. She also heard the message at church that sex was "nasty" and that good girls would never put themselves in a compromising position. Those messages were brought into her marriage, and she let the bad habit of not expressing her desires develop because she felt shameful even talking about sex, let alone enjoying it. Whenever she got close to enjoying sex, guilt would take over and shut down the process. The husband was oblivious to the fact that his wife was turning over and crying after sex because she felt so unsatisfied.

Fortunately, we were able to fix their problem. Once the floodgates opened and they could talk in a neutral environment, not in bed, the wife could tell her husband that she needed more foreplay and that she was also interested in introducing a toy into their sex play. She explained that she was so worried about how long it was taking her to orgasm because of the prolonged effort she was causing him to endure. She felt if they added the toy as an enhancement, it would help them both; he wouldn't have to work as hard and she wouldn't worry about him working hard.

Add to that a great lubricant and a night away from the kids and—*voilà!*—she had her first orgasm. Of course, they had to communicate throughout the process and be honest about what felt good. Most importantly, they kept up the new, good communication habits rather than falling back into old patterns of "why can't he read my mind" and getting frustrated when it doesn't happen. She learned to allow herself to feel pleasure and acknowledge that she was worthy of it.

Baggage Guilt

Another type of guilt I see is baggage guilt. For example, a young woman grows up in a home where Christian values have been taught. Her parents and church expect her not to have sex before marriage. The problem: she did have sex before marriage. Even if she followed her religious teachings and sought forgiveness, she still carries that memory with her. I have known so many women like this. Some tell their husbands of their previous indiscretions; some keep it secret. Both of these approaches can cause suffering, because they feel that they are bringing past baggage into the marriage.

Some women even feel guilty because they enjoyed their old flings and now feel shame for unintentionally comparing their routine marital sex to their previous "naughty" sex. This is especially true if a woman's husband was chaste prior to marriage. This can be particularly challenging to resolve if the guilt-burdened partner refuses to let go of the past. Therapy may or may not help, but it's hoped that as a couple experiences their own sexual adventures, these will gradually replace old experiences with new, better ones.

The concept of baggage guilt is a little more complex than the name implies, but it's important to understand its implications. It's more than just bringing past experiences into a relationship. It's bringing them into the current sexual engagement and allowing them to impact the current experience in mixed ways. I call it "baggage/guilt" ("baggage-slash-guilt") because it can often be that the person is deciding between one or the other. I can best explain this through a couple of stories.

Erik and Alyssa had been married for three years and were in their early 20s. When he was a teenager, he had masturbated a couple times a week on average. Now married and beyond what they considered to be the honeymoon phase, he had returned to masturbating in secrecy. His wife had caught him, and they ended up sitting in my office.

This story is not unusual, especially for young Christian couples, and there are many things that can be gleaned from it, but allow me to share an important concept from Erik and Alyssa's experience. Like many young Christian men, Erik had significant guilt over his masturbation (whole books can be written on that topic, and in fact they have been). He had expected that once he was married and free to have intercourse, his desire for masturbation would subside. In early marriage, it did somewhat; but after a few months of marriage, he found himself returning to masturbation more than he had expected, and because of the newlyweds' inability to communicate about masturbation, he relieved himself in secrecy.

He had developed an overwhelming conflict of emotions: the pleasure of masturbation, coupled with his unmet expectation that intercourse would relieve him of that desire, combined with regret for having started the act as a teen. Not to mention that he was keeping this all from his wife. The guilt he felt wasn't just about the "old baggage" he had brought into the relationship, but that his baggage was still a source of pleasure in the present and that it was affecting his current relationship.

Let's see if another example makes this clearer.

Wendy was referred to me by her minister after she had visited with him regarding some marriage struggles she and her husband were having. During counseling, she confessed to repeatedly having watched some fairly obscene pornography prior to her marriage and having been aroused by it. She now found it difficult to become aroused and orgasm with her husband as they engaged in relatively mild sex. She and her husband had decided to hold to their current values and not allow pornography to be part of their marriage, so she had repented of her prior pornography viewing, but her sex life was suffering as a result.

In this case, she relieved herself of the guilt, yet the baggage of the past was interfering with the present. She knew that if she allowed herself to watch some of that same pornography again, it would reinvigorate her libido and enflame her passions, yet she was reluctant to suggest that to her husband or even to consider it for herself privately. It took time, but as she was counseled by her minister and me, she eventually learned to prioritize sensual intimacy over sexual arousal. Eventually, as she and her husband deepened their interpersonal intimacy, she was able to achieve sexual satisfaction from their loving relationship rather than having to shock her libido into overdrive using extreme sexual fantasies.

A final story is that of Brenda. She was in her mid-30s and married for less than a year to her husband. As a teenager, she had been fairly wild with multiple sex partners—male and female—then as a young adult, she became abstinent and more pious with hopes of finding a sweet husband. But during this time, she masturbated a few times a month on average. She did not consider this to be a violation of her abstinence promise to herself, and she was living what she considered to be the life of a devoted and faithful Christian.

She married her husband more than ten years after her last sexual encounter. She wasn't even a year into marriage before she found me. She admitted to me that she often fantasized about her past sexual experiences (mostly, but not always, the ones involving women) while she was having sex with her husband. She felt horrible guilt, but it also brought her tremendous sexual satisfaction. She loved her husband dearly and had no desire for a change in their sexual relationship. She found him attractive and skillful and attentive. She just felt guilty about bringing baggage into the relationship that she felt ought not to be there.

∽○∾

In each of these examples, there was secrecy—partially out of frustration with one's self, but also out of fear of how one's partner may respond. The secrecy may also be because the individuals don't want to admit how their past "surmounted" sexual experiences still appeal to them. They are torn between what they *should* feel and what they *do* feel. They *did* get pleasure from their past sexual experience, and those experiences (the "baggage") are still tantalizing to them now, and they feel guilty now about the "kinky" pleasures their bodies crave.

Dealing with baggage guilt isn't easy. Couples often enlist the help of their pastor or a marriage therapist to help them understand and overcome their internal conflicts, and when the conflict is so great that it's causing distress, I support these paths. Others find it helpful to not continually dredge up the past by trying to pick apart the source of their struggles, but rather to just move forward by trying something new, and that is what I often propose to couples.

This is what worked for Erik and Alyssa. Once Alyssa was over the initial shock of discovering that her husband frequently masturbated, I could help her understand that most men masturbate, even while enjoying a happy sexual relationship with their partner. Rather than continuing to dwell on the psychological undertones, I had them start on some of the mutual touching exercises in this book. This allowed Erik to show his wife what he liked and it helped Alyssa understand that there were a variety of ways in which her husband received sexual pleasure. As Alyssa better understood and accepted some of her husband's desires, he felt less guilty about bringing his interests into their relationship.

Teaching couples new terms like "sensual touch" or "mutual satisfaction" and turning away from the negativity of the word "masturbation" helped not only this couple, but many others. I find it important to help men understand that a big part of the "hurt" that women feel regarding masturbation is the idea that she, as your partner, isn't good enough, when in fact it comes down to a communication problem. Women are naturally pleasers; we like our partners to be happy. Teach us! It may seem embarrassing or unnatural, but once you work through the roadblocks, it is well worth the effort.

Overcoming guilt isn't easy, and it takes a lot of time, but it can be done. Whether or not you choose to enlist the aid of a minister or marriage counselor, it is important that you enlist the aid of your spouse. By communicating with one another, and learning to forgive and be forgiven, you can move forward in your marriage. That is not to say that the baggage guilt may be completely removed, but you can move beyond it as a couple and start fresh.

Pious Guilt

I would call this "religious" guilt, but I would hope that no one's actual religious doctrine attempts to shame married couples who enjoy marital sex, so I call this "pious" guilt, or I could equally refer to this as "religious-cultural" guilt. As someone who talks and thinks about sex a lot, I have had people in my community attempt to shame me for doing what I do—some explicitly, some more subtly—and it's often done under the pretext of religious shame, but in actuality, it's their personal interpretation.

Forms of this type of guilt are probably the most common that I see: having "impure thoughts," guilt over touching one's genitals or their partner's, guilt over focusing too much on sex, and the list goes on. And each one of these is backed by an interpretation of a scripture, a supposed teaching, a rumor, an allegory, or an admonition.

Some interpretations of religious teachings may give some validity to the attempted shaming, but the needless, ineffectual, and destructive guilt that we religious people feel over sex has at times escalated to the point of pleasure paralysis. And we as individual recipients share the blame, because we allow a haughty look to wither us and make us blush. I realize that that may be simplistic, but my advice to couples is this: figure out if you've sinned. If you have, repent and move on. If you haven't, then don't give it a second thought. If you're not sure, then hurry up; stop wasting your life, and figure it out quick!

Communication Guilt

Communication guilt would probably be better named "lack-of-communication guilt." Consider the three people that I described in the Baggage Guilt section: Erik, Wendy, and Brenda. Each of them kept a secret from their spouse, and we can probably understand why—they feared the consequences of sharing. They feared the injury, loss, or pain that could occur to their spouses—and subsequently to themselves—if they confessed their sexual secrets. For Wendy, who still recalled sexual fantasies even during her happy marriage, she found it helpful and satisfying to share with her husband some of her more mild fantasies and have them role-play. This allowed her to open up to her husband and for him to better understand what drives her sexuality without her having to expose him to her entire past.

Most people wish they could confess their lusty desires to their partners, and that even if their partners didn't respond with enthusiasm, there would at least be understanding, acceptance, and comfort. But the reality is that some partners don't respond that way, so the secret-keeper decides to keep the desires (past and/or present) buried to protect the status quo. This can cause another layer of guilt—guilt for not being open and honest, guilt for not allowing their partner to participate in the truth, guilt for every moment that the truth is buried. If this is you, you may feel ready to burst. But before you do, consider the next type of guilt.

Exposé Guilt

Once you share something, you can't take it back. In most cases, I support sharing of feelings and thoughts. But I don't make those decisions for you. I don't tell clients what to do. I ask you what you're *going to do,* and then coach you along the process that you've set for yourself. So, as I stated, if a person is ready to share with their partner their sexual secret, I support it and guide the process along, but that doesn't mean that I haven't seen this sharing end in pain.

I commend the man who reveals his secret sexual desires to his wife. While it may be met with a little hiccup, most people are glad to get it out in the open and work through it. A little time passes, and things are usually much better than before. But that's not always the case. Some partners just won't accept the news, and things spiral downward. And then the guilt sets in. The husband who felt guilty about his prior acts, then felt guilty about not confessing to his wife, now feels that he's made a mistake by confessing and further harming the relationship. Even if he later agrees that all these steps were inevitable, he still feels pain with each step.

As I said, I can't make the decision for you about whether or not to share a secret with your partner. Though I support open communication in any relationship, it is up to you to weigh the pros and cons of sharing and to decide for yourself how to proceed. But if you are on the receiving end of a revelation like this, do your best to be open and understanding in order to minimize friction in your relationship, and to reduce your partner's guilt. Most likely, they have punished themselves enough as it is; don't add to it.

Gender-Role Guilt

Gender-role guilt is a tricky issue for many women, especially those who come from conservative backgrounds. I have seen many women who come to me with a similar story to my client Jennifer. Like many people I've worked with, Jennifer grew up in a highly religious Catholic home, where sex was rarely talked about. If it was discussed, she was told that it was the woman's job to "lie there and provide for her husband."

She also became ashamed of her body because she constantly heard the message that all boys wanted was sex, and that's all they looked at women for. The shame came with her conflicting feelings about the message her female relatives taught and the actual desire she had to be sexual. She felt that there must be something wrong with her because she enjoyed her sexuality.

It became a big hurdle in her marriage because she really did enjoy sex. She liked making her husband happy and loved to orgasm. However, the guilt she felt about enjoying sex soon overpowered her desire to have a healthy sex life. She knew that there had to be something wrong with her. Sadly, this led to a difficult patch in her marriage.

Her husband, Adam, who had enjoyed sex with his wife, was suddenly being rejected at every advance. Worse, Jennifer would give in "to fulfill her wifely duty" only once or twice a month at best. These sexual encounters quickly became unfulfilling for Jennifer's husband. He could tell she wasn't enjoying sex and felt like it was simply a checkmark on her to-do list.

You can guess what happened next. A few advances from a work associate and Adam found himself in a place he never imagined. Soon after, I met the couple in my office. Jennifer was devastated. Adam was fighting hard to salvage his marriage. He deeply loved his wife and was willing to do anything to fight for his family.

After a few emotional and difficult sessions, Adam was able to honestly explain how empty sex had become. He explained to Jennifer how much he missed the sexy, confident wife he had married. Jennifer was also able to open up about how guilty she felt about enjoying sex and her concern that a woman and mom shouldn't be having "such a good time." It wasn't a quick or easy path to build back the trust after Adam's infidelity; however, Jennifer decided to work on herself during the process.

She tried hard to break down the taboo that had affected her sexual attitude. She also realized that she didn't want to pass the same message on to her children. She worked on feeling sexy again, and that in turn strengthened her relationship with Adam. He loved his wife's new attitude and found it to be a huge turn-on. This only added to Jennifer's confidence and strengthened her resolve. They also learned how important honesty and communication are in a marriage, no matter how hard it may seem.

Of course, the ideal is for neither partner to get to the point of infidelity, and I don't condone Adam's decision to cheat on his wife. Unfortunately, this is an all-too-familiar scenario. Women need to remember that men love sexually confident partners. I have never known a man who doesn't love and find pride in watching his wife orgasm. It's much sexier than a partner who is having sex just to put a check in the box.

When women are taught that their role in a sexual relationship is just to fulfill a duty, to check the box, it teaches that sex should not be enjoyed. This is completely false. It is the role of both partners to find pleasure in sex and joy in pleasing one another.

Performance Guilt

This section may be better titled "lack-of-performance guilt." One may think this is primarily a woman's issue—for example, the woman who can't orgasm, so she starts down the path of faking. Eventually, she starts to feel resentment that her husband cannot read her mind and see that she isn't truly enjoying sex. This in turn results in the woman avoiding sex and her husband becoming frustrated with her lack of intimacy. It usually comes to a head when the woman cannot take it anymore and finally admits that she has never been, or rarely is, satisfied during sex.

This problem, however, is a big issue with men, too. A man may suddenly find himself unable to get or keep an erection. Rather than explain this to his wife, he will withdraw from the sexual relationship. This often leaves the wife thinking his rejections are her fault. Is she not thin enough, pretty enough, sexy enough? Is it that she has stretch marks, baby weight, or wrinkles? Or worse, is he having an affair? This, of course, can drive an even larger wedge between the couple.

Often, erection issues can be related to medical issues and medications. But many of the same issues that affect women being able to orgasm also affect men. What society doesn't talk about is that a man may simply be tired, stressed, or disconsolate from a bad day at work and suddenly find himself unable to perform; the media certainly doesn't teach that this is normal.

Communication is key in fixing this type of guilt. If a woman isn't achieving an orgasm during sex, she needs to be honest with her partner. He cannot read the woman's mind! She needs to learn to tell him what feels good and what isn't working. Often, women do not even know what they like. She must learn what feels good to her and know how her body responds so she can teach her partner.

A man also needs to learn to be comfortable enough to communicate with his partner when he is having a rough day. The worst thing a loving partner can do is tear the man down or make him feel guilty about the situation. This leads down an even more destructive path that is hard to come back from.

A conservative lifestyle, while commendable, can also be a breeding ground for guilt. Far too often, in conservative circles, young adults receive heavy-handed lessons on chastity and modesty that have negative fallout down the road. I see conservative parents and religious instructors patting themselves on the back for preaching morality, but ignoring the disastrous effects these lessons have as they breed guilt about sex in perfectly moral people. To be true examples and teachers of morality, we can't just merely throw the lesson out there and leave it be; we should also monitor the effects our lessons have to ensure that we are not only creating moral youths, but sexually empowered adults.

Chapter 4
=====

Communication

When people ask me, "What's the key to great sex?" I tell them that it's oral—they have to use their mouth and speak to their partner, and then their partner has to offer that same oral service. Whether you're getting married next week or have been married for 50 years, the best way to make sex better is to talk about it. Nothing else comes close to beating that—not a new position, not lingerie, not even *Seinfeld's* infamous swirl.

A willingness to talk about sex—or at least a desire to be willing to talk about it—is absolutely critical to improving one's sex life. Despite this grand key, I see countless couples that are profoundly uncomfortable discussing their sexuality. They can bicker about all sorts of things, but in their sex lives, silence reigns. These people never discuss what they like and dislike in the bedroom, what feels especially good, and what turns them on.

I start off telling you this because I know that most couples who have sexual challenges actually have sexual communication challenges. I don't expect that my just saying this is going to fix the problem; I say this so that you'll keep it in mind as you undertake the process that this book presents. If you follow along and do the exercises, the communication will follow. By the end of this book, you'll both be so open to talking about sex that you're going to have to start being cognizant of who might be listening to you!

If you're like the 95 percent of couples who don't communicate well about sex, you're hoping that as long as you live good lives and are in love, your sex lives will magically be amazing. These couples go into marriage as if in a fairy tale: they've married their prince or princess, and now it's time for the "sexily ever after," and they're disappointed when their relationship doesn't sizzle like they think it ought to.

There's really no other aspect of our lives that we approach like this. Imagine wanting to build your dream house. You've saved up enough money. You've located the perfect plot of land. You've found an architect, and you're ready to start work. Would you then think to yourself, "I don't need to discuss my ideas with my architect. I'm a good person, and he should just know what I want. I'm sure that things will work out and my home will be great"?

That's nuts, right? Everyone's idea of the perfect house is different. For one person, it may be a ten-bedroom villa. For another, it may be a small summer cottage surrounded by orchards and gardens. No matter how good an architect is, he can't read your mind. If you want something, you need to express it.

Similarly, what is "good sex" to one person might be bizarre to another. The development of sexual tastes is a complicated process that involves a lot of factors, including one's family, upbringing, experiences, culture, religion, and gender. Very few spouses have identical sexual desires. But if you never talk about sex with your partner, you may erroneously assume that your sexual dreams and goals are more similar than they truly are. This can lead to times when sex inexplicably "just goes wrong," which then leads to tension and frustration.

I received a phone call from Juan, who mentioned he and his wife lived out of state, but that he would do whatever was necessary to fix his marriage. He was clearly upset and a bit nervous speaking to me. I quickly learned that his was not an unfamiliar story. He and his wife had been married many years—decades. Suddenly, out of the blue, Juan's wife informed him that she had never enjoyed sex in their marriage and in fact had never had an orgasm.

She was extremely frustrated and felt it was too late in their marriage to ever change. Juan was devastated, not only at the potential loss of the marriage, but that he hadn't been satisfying his wife throughout their married life. I suggested that we make an appointment to discuss the situation further.

They came into San Antonio for the weekend and we meet on a Friday afternoon. It was immediately obvious how much love there was between them. Equally obvious was their frustration in communicating their feelings in a helpful way. Sex is a sensitive subject! It needs to be discussed in a calm, peaceful, and positive environment.

When Juan and Maria arrived in my office, it was clear Maria had become very frustrated and hurt over the decades of unmet sexual needs. Juan was equally as frustrated with the situation. He loved his wife dearly but didn't know how to help her communicate her desires.

The first thing to remember in a situation similar to this is that you don't discuss sexual deficiencies in the middle of sex! These talks are best over pancakes the next morning. Also, never start the conversation with hurtful words or a list of all your partner needs to do to improve. Chances are that is one of the reasons you got to where you are in the first place; communication failed, so one or both partners stopped trying.

Luckily for this couple, all it took was the safe environment of my office, along with a weekend away, to help Maria find her voice. To her surprise, Juan loved that she was finally telling him what she liked. This gave her more courage to speak up and in turn gave Juan more joy in satisfying his wife. It was no longer about just taking care of his own needs and turning over to go to sleep; he made sure *she* was happy first. Maria was so excited to finally be orgasming, and her only disappointment was that it had taken her so many years to speak up.

So why don't couples talk about sex? A common reason is because it would expose our vulnerability. Sexual desires rest near to our heart—so near that we sometimes don't even admit them to ourselves. They're complicated, and we can be equally drawn to and repulsed by them. They're illogical and beyond rational justification. We don't know why we want something—we just know we want it. Because of all this, it can be especially hard to let a spouse in and admit the things that we crave. We may fear mockery and judgment.

Similarly, we may feel embarrassed when talking about it. When growing up, many of us learned that sex was taboo, and that sexual topics merited only whispers and blushes. But you're now an adult, and the time has come to let go of childish feelings. Get over it. Once you're in the bedroom with your spouse, being bashful isn't helpful or attractive. You must get used to saying words like "penis" and "vagina." Get accustomed to saying things like, "I like it when you rub the top of my clitoris."

Learn to describe the things that you want to do and want done to you (once you learn what you want). As you do this, you will find that something wonderful happens. Not only will your partner know how to pleasure you, you will also find yourself coming more to terms with your own sexuality. When you shed sexual embarrassment, you will feel happier and closer to each other.

I'll give you one more pearl: When it comes to talking about sex, sex acts themselves are forms of communication. The way you touch your partner, the way you look into each other's eyes, and the way you kiss are all expressions of your love for each other and celebrating your relationship. This is part of the reason why romance stories often include a sex scene—it's another way to indicate that the couple is in love.

Because sex works on a level deeper than words, it can be one of the most powerful, visceral, and beautiful ways to communicate with one another. In time, your sexual experiences will allow you to say things to each other that your words cannot. But before you can communicate with your bodies, you need to start at the beginning and learn to communicate with your words.

Exercise: The List

This exercise will help you and your partner establish or strengthen your sexual communication. It may be helpful to read over this assignment alone first before presenting it to your spouse. You should both be aware that you're not going to be allowed to see each other's list. (Have a shredder or matches ready.)

First, each of you separately write down a list of things you like or would like to try sexually. Make your list thorough, and write what *you* like, not what you think your partner expects or what you feel you ought to like. This can take some bravery and self-discovery. You can put anything you'd like on your list.

Next, rank each item on a scale of 1 to 10 for its "shock value." A 1 is something that is very tame, and a 10 means it's something that could be very abhorrent to your partner.

Once you're done numbering, sit down with your spouse, but don't look at each other's list. Take turns sharing, starting with items that are marked as 1s, then gauge the response you get from your partner. If your partner also made a list, let them take a turn. Keep going back and forth down the list as you become more daring with each item you share. You don't need to state that an item is a 4 or a 7; just keep getting more and more daring as you share.

It may be helpful if you both acknowledge that there are items on the list that you may not end up sharing at this time. If you do share everything on the list and neither of you has run from the room, you have an amazing relationship, can toss this book aside, and jump into bed. But it's not unusual for couples to sense some discomfort before getting to the 7s. If things get uncomfortable, stop. Now's the time to burn the unread portions of your lists.

I hope that by this point you've divulged some things that are new, and even if your disclosure wasn't completely accepted, your spouse now has an idea of some of your sexual interests, and this will make it easier to try when the moment is right. Similarly, I hope that you were able to tolerate learning something new about your partner's desires and that you'll be more willing to make adjustments. Do this exercise every year and see how your sexual relationship grows!

Chapter 5

Sexy and Empowered

I'd like to have a moment alone with the women. Guys, take five. Your wives are about to learn what it means to feel and be sexy. You men can return just before the end of the chapter, when I have a short section for the guys.

Now that we're alone, ladies, let's have a little heart-to-heart. I assume that your guy loves you and is devoted to you. I assume that he's a good man who cares for you. If this isn't the case, it may be time for a heart-to-heart conversation with him and/or a counselor.

Even if he provides for your family, takes little Jordan to her soccer games and little Ashton to his piano lessons, and goes to church with you on Sundays, that's not necessarily the same as having sexual intimacy in your relationship, is it? I certainly hope that you do have the spark of romance in your relationship—that he kisses you like a lover, not like your children's mother; that you see the passion in his eyes when he pulls you in close. I hope that when he comes home from work, he whispers to you that he couldn't get you out of his mind all day. I hope that he spends his days thinking about how to seduce you and his nights dreaming about you.

Sounds nice, doesn't it? Well, I'm here to tell you that you *should* have that in your life. You should have romance and passion, and we're going to discuss how to make it happen. And before you start protesting that you aren't 18 anymore, or that you don't have model proportions, I'm going to tell you that it doesn't matter. You can have this whether you're slim or curvaceous, whether you're 22 or 62, whether your hair is brown, blonde, or white. It is possible!

To be this woman, you may have to make some changes. I'm not talking about liposuction and hair extensions—that's easy, and not as effective as the media would make you believe. I'm talking about how you think and act. I'm talking about waking up your inner *femme*. I'm talking about embracing the sensuality and sexuality that are at your very core as a woman.

Notice that I'm not saying that you have to *create* sexuality, sensuality, or sexiness. I'm telling you that these attributes are your innate, God-given birthright, which even if they have been squelched, still exist somewhere in you. All you have to do is find them, acknowledge them, and exercise them.

First, recognize that you are a human female, and as such, you are innately sexual—your body was built for sex. The next step in making this change is giving yourself permission to pursue the "sexy." I see it over and over: women are their own worst enemies and most destructive critics. As women, we must let go of self-sabotaging thoughts. In order to delve to the deepest recesses of your sexual being, you must for the moment ignore messages that would try to convince you that such self-evaluation is impermissible. Ignore the pessimistic voices saying that you can't do this; ignore the defeatist voices saying that you'll never be good enough, so why try; and ignore the shaming voices that tell you it's just plain wrong. In the end, all they have to offer is insecurity, immaturity, and embarrassment.

On the other hand, there are some very compelling reasons why you ought to discover your inner sensual core. It's what you were designed for. You were built for sex. That's why all the parts work the way they do, and why men don't need to be taught to be attracted to women. It's just something built into the very nature of what it means to be human.

Also, pursuing sex is fun! You have the opportunity to turn his head in a way that you perhaps never have, and there's nothing quite like the ego-rush that you get when you've made your man wild with adoration. The power to reduce him to awestruck wonder is an amazing feeling, to feel as though you're the only woman in the world to him. And your man will love this, too. Being with you will be the high point of his day, and he'll wonder how in the world he could have gotten so lucky as to end up married to you. And this will make your marriage stronger, more vibrant, and exciting.

When you add it all up, there are far more reasons to accept being sexy than not, so why not give it a try?

Sexiness Matters

Donna was seeing me because she felt like she and her husband were growing apart, and she was worried because he was being friendlier with women at church than Donna had seen in the past. Her husband had always been shy, but now she was noticing that he was more outgoing, and she worried that it could lead to something. I had not met her husband, but she gave me permission to speak to him by phone the night before this follow-up session with her. I had called him that night and we had a very enlightening conversation.

Donna started this session reiterating her ongoing concerns and expressed that she'd hoped that I was able to convince her husband to do the right thing and focus more on their marriage and less on others. After letting her say her piece, I kindly informed her, "The problem isn't your husband. It's you." I told her that I believed that her husband wasn't being unfaithful to her, but that because she had ceased making an effort to maintain his attraction, he was naturally being attracted elsewhere.

I told her husband that if he's feeling less attracted to his wife, he owes it to her to tell her and to tell her why. He, like most husbands, was terrified to think what would happen if he said that to her. What would *you* do if your husband said that to you? Would you rather he not say anything and just quietly (maybe subconsciously) turn his attention elsewhere?

Men crave sex. If you have a problem with that, take it up with God and nature, because that's how they're designed. If you're aware of *The Five Love Languages*, I don't think it would be much of an overstatement to say that, for many men, sex is its own love language, and for some men, it's the one that rules them all!

Ladies, if you want your husband to feel attracted to you, you must attract him. Doing otherwise is just playing games with him. It's not fair that now that you've put a ring on his finger, you think you can get as frumpy as you want and then test his fidelity. That's like buying a dog, not feeding it or playing with it, and then getting mad at it when it runs away or dies.

To a man, sex means so much more to him than you may realize, and he may not even consciously know how important it is to him. It combines his favorite emotional and physical aspects of your relationship with the most enjoyable hobby in the world. Sex means love, security, validation, intimacy, pleasure, and relief. For him, sex is like taking the best and most meaningful aspects of your relationship and combining them into the most wonderful outlet possible.

There are a variety of reasons why men crave sex emotionally. Men are expected to be self-sufficient, independent, intellectual, and in control of their feelings. Sex is one of the few times in their lives when they're able to let down their barriers, to be vulnerable, and to be in touch with their bodies and feelings.

Sex also provides a means for men to experience the comforting power of touch—we all need this for our emotional health. But American culture is not comfortable addressing male touch; whether in business settings or social gatherings, men who excessively touch are treated with suspicion and distrust. Because of this, sex remains one of the few places where men can be allowed to give and receive touch.

Just as men need sex on an emotional level, they also crave it on a physical level. From the time that they hit adolescence, feeling "horny" is something that most men experience on a daily basis. Most men learn to bridle it, yet still have that itch yearning for a scratch. Without sexual release, men can become twitchy, withdrawn, and crabby.

So, given that men have this incredible sex drive, what are we to do with it? Some women treat it as a nuisance, as something that disrupts their sleep and puts a burden on their time. Some women distrust it and watch their husbands jealously for potential glances at other women. But I'll tell you the real secret: your husband's sex drive may be your greatest resource for keeping him madly, desperately, passionately in love with you. Express your sexiness and you'll keep your man coming to you again and again. Each encounter will simultaneously satiate and inflame him in a virtuous cycle of love and passion.

In this regard, good sex is one of the best ways that you can strengthen your relationship. If you have frequent, enthusiastic sex, he will associate feelings of pleasure and longing with you. On the other hand, if you are routinely unavailable, disinterested, or begrudging, his concept of sexiness will naturally be diverted elsewhere, even if just in thought. Take pride and enjoyment in sex, and you will see the dividends in your relationship.

As a Woman Thinketh

Men are visual creatures; I'm sure that's not news to you. But their libidos are affected by more than just looking at a pair of perky breasts. I had a male client tell me once that the quickest way for a stripper to crush his desire is for her to start talking. As harsh as this example is, it highlights an important aspect of a man's libido: his sexual desire is genuinely affected by a woman's expressions of desire for him. If she is flighty, distracted, begrudging, stressed, or apathetic, all the lingerie in the world won't make up for it.

Consider this in regard to pornography. It's not just the physical appearance that arouses him, but also the fact that the woman in the image doesn't bring any mental baggage to the "engagement." Because the woman on the page (or stripper on the pole) is essentially a fictional character, the man can subconsciously impose any mental scenario his id can create in order to best facilitate his sexual desires. Admittedly, this imaginary relationship can only run so deep and will only bring very limited sexual satisfaction. In a real-life, committed relationship, the sexual reward can be many times greater, but this will be achieved only as both partners develop the appropriate attitudes toward female sexuality.

I have fortunately found a few examples of healthy sexuality in the media. While 99 percent of the media makes a woman feel she must be blonde, 5'10", 110 pounds, and built like a volleyball player, I'm pleased that we're now seeing examples of sexually empowered women who don't fit the "ideal" physical mold. One example on TV is that of an overweight female lawyer, who is essentially the reincarnation of a deceased fashion model. Her body size and shape have not crushed her strong, sexy attitude. Because she spent her former life in the spotlight, she still *thinks* she's sexy, so she *acts* sexy, and therefore she *is* sexy.

I know women like this in real life—women who refuse to fit the mold, no matter how large that mold is. They *believe* they are sexy, and so they are. And we've all met women who are the exact opposite of this: gorgeous women who focus on the smallest blemish to the annoyance of those around them. It's hard to think a woman is attractive if she doesn't find herself attractive.

Let's talk about the word "sexy" for a minute. I have found that many women have a problem with this word. They associate it with inappropriate behavior and dress and "bad girls." I remind women that some synonyms of "sexy" are "amorous," "desirable," "seductive," "sensual," "flirtatious," "inviting," "covetable," "enticing," "beautiful," and "alluring." I don't know any women who wouldn't want to feel at least one of those emotions.

Unfortunately, the media has done a very good job of making the word "sexy" salacious, dirty, and "naughty." We need to take sexy back. It's okay to feel sexy, be sexy, and act sexy. A sexy woman is strong and empowered. A sexy woman walks with confidence and commands a room. She feels flirtatious, desirable, and beautiful.

She's Got the Look

If you're willing to change your attitude and consider the possibility that you can think like a sexy woman, it's time to give some outward support for your newfound sexual understanding. Men can try to overcome this desire, but they are aroused by what they see, so why not work with it rather than fight an uphill battle?

Seeing you dressed sexily is often all it takes to get him aroused and in the mood. On the other hand, if a woman makes no effort to appear attractive, no matter how much he loves her, it can make his arousal a challenge for him. If you really want to light his fire, baggy sweatpants may not always cut it.

I'm going to offer general guidance on how to look sexy. And it's likely the same message that you get hundreds of times a day from countless advertisers. But before you just start buying new lipstick, coloring your hair, and trying on skirts, let's slow down and consider how you're going to decide how to improve your appearance. Try this: *ask him!*

What would happen if you asked your husband what you could do to be more physically attractive to him? (I bet your mind just went racing!) How he answers says a lot about your relationship. If he says, "Nothing, Dear. You look beautiful just the way you are," he could be sincere, or he could be terrified of the consequences of saying anything other than that. Which is it? Or maybe you're too terrified to ask him the question for fear of what he could say. That's another sign that your communication level isn't where it should be. So, maybe you can't ask a question as broad as that, but you can ask, "Which of these lipsticks do you like better?" and then wear the one he picks.

I once went with my husband to get his hair cut. The barber asked him how he'd like it cut, and my husband said, "Ask her. She's the one that has to look at it. I only see it in the mirror once a day." He was willing to put my interests ahead of his. Regarding my hair, my husband has confessed that he likes me to have long hair. For the most part, I don't mind long hair, but there are some summers in San Antonio when I just want to shave it bald, and he knows if I cut my hair short that my need for comfort will have overtaken his desires.

The point here is that we both know what's going on in each other's minds. I know what he finds attractive because I've asked him. I know that he likes me in stiletto heels. I know that turns him on. But he knows that my feet occasionally hurt, and he understands why I can't wear them all the time. He knows the sacrifice that I make for him when I do wear them, and I expect him to verbally recognize my effort. (See all the explicit communication we're having?)

So before I start giving you generic advice on how you could start looking sexier, you need to understand who you're doing it for. You're doing it for a lot of people: yourself, your spouse, your family, your colleagues, your friends, the public, etc. Because you do not live on a deserted island, you can't just dress for yourself. Your choice of appearance conveys a message about how you feel about yourself and how you want others to feel about you. And because you can't change your appearance 30 times a day for every person you encounter, you'll need to strike a balance that works for you.

If you care about no one's opinion (and have low self-esteem), maybe pajamas and flip-flops are all you need. If you're most concerned about the people at church, then keep everything covered. But if your priority is your marriage, then you need to find out what your marriage needs, and apart from doing a whole lot of expensive trial and error, the only way to do that is to talk about it with him, and the exercise on page 74 will help you two get there.

Dress to Impress

Do you remember how you dressed when you were dating? You probably picked your outfits carefully, trying to show that you were interested. You likely wanted to accentuate some features and mask others. Compare that to now. When you're getting dressed, do you pick clothes that make you feel attractive? Often, once married, some women settle into wearing comfort clothes more than wearing attractive outfits. Consciously or subconsciously, this may be because they have already gotten their man and they don't need to win him over again.

Spouses that have this attitude are saying that their relationship is so strong that it can withstand a lack of maintenance. It may be true, but this attitude also shows a dispassion for the relationship's importance. The key message here is this: know what your spouse needs to continually feel attracted to you, and if you don't know, then talk about it!

My general advice is to dress sexy. Whether you're playing the role of mother, daughter, boss, or sister, these don't preclude you from looking sexy—whatever that phrase means to you and your spouse. Look at your wardrobe. What does it say to you? What does it say to him? Does it say "mom"? Being a mother is wonderful, but I'll tell you right now that if that's the first thing your husband thinks when he looks at you, there may be better ways to get him turned on. You want his first thought to be "Wow!"

For those women who might be concerned that I'm telling them to dress slutty, I'm not. In fact, I'm not telling you to change anything. I'm telling you to think about your own standards of what sexy means to you and what sexy means to him, and if you don't know what sexy means to him, ask! If you can both honestly say that your current wardrobe is sexy, then you're doing great and can skip to the next chapter, but if you discover some areas in which to improve, then my goal is achieved.

The Sexy Wardrobe

Every few years, we women need something of a wardrobe makeover. We tend to hold onto clothes that emphasize function over form. We have clothes that we've held onto for far too long. Sometimes we don't even remember why we bought them in the first place. Step One in having a sexier wardrobe is getting rid of the things that aren't sexy.

You're going to get rid of anything that is ripped, stained, or completely worn through. Donate to your local charity, make a quilt out of it, or make it into rags, but don't keep it in your closet where you'll be tempted to wear it. You're going to keep no more than one or two sets of "comfort clothes," because we all have days when we just need to let our hair down and be comfortable. However, if there are too many of those days, you'll notice that you're wearing the same two outfits over and over, or you'll get out of your slump and put on something enticing!

Next, get rid of the clothes that you have "just because." We each have had clothes that don't flatter us and maybe don't flatter anyone! Get rid of those, too. If they make you feel frumpy and you don't like them, why do you have them? Maybe someone else will find them sexy, but you certainly won't.

Culling your wardrobe may leave you with less than half of what you started with, but what remains should make you feel very attractive! And it will make room for something new and stylish.

When you dress so that you feel sexy, you will find that it increases his level of attraction to you, and that will boost your confidence. And as I said before, confidence is the ultimate aphrodisiac.

A Note on Modesty

There are a good number of women reading this who are going to say that I am promoting immodesty. Please reread the above section and note that I made no mention of the length of skirt you should buy or the size of top you should wear. Modesty is an incredibly vague and subjective term and should always be combined with the qualifier of "...according to whom?" Because you live and move through many microcultures each day (work, church, school, home, bedroom), you can be modest and immodest at the same time, depending on who's making the call.

So before you start thinking about being modest or not, you need to decide on who you're going to allow to be your judge. If you're going to be more concerned about Mrs. Busy-Body-Church-Lady's looks of scorn than your husband's looks of delight, then it's going to be difficult to make a change.

Hygiene

This should go without saying, but for some, it needs to be said. Stay clean and smelling nice. If the smell of sweat is a turn-on in your relationship, be sure to let each other know. Otherwise, assume that it's not, and take a soapy shower. Our sense of smell is strongly tied to our most basic emotions and can have subconscious implications on our relationship.

Consider the way you feel when you haven't showered for two days. Your hair is a little greasy, and you just feel dirty. It's unlikely that you feel sexy when you're in this state. Being clean and well groomed will increase your confidence and help you to feel sexy. Don't overlook this.

Discuss grooming preferences with your mate. Do you like him to have a smooth face? Does he like you to have shaved legs? And what about grooming the nether regions[6]? As always, communicating about your preferences will yield the best results for your efforts.

Talk the Talk

We've already discussed the importance of communication about sex, but it deserves repeating. Being sexy means that you can talk about sex. If you're like me, you may get to the point where you have to guard against talking about it too much. Not everyone around you wants to hear about it. But when you're with your spouse, especially when you're *alone* with your spouse, you should be able to say anything you

---

6   I'm using euphemisms for now to ease you into it, but eventually we need to use the real words for anatomy and sex acts in order to avoid confusion.

want about sex using any language you want. Words that you'd never utter in mixed company should be allowed and encouraged between the two of you. You share a unique and private relationship, so you should have your own private language that you reserve for just the two of you.

Female Empowerment

Despite the great strides made in gender equality, most of us were raised to be quiet, demure, and passive, especially in the bedroom. Unfortunately, that does both us and our husbands a disservice. Most of the men I've talked to wish that their wives were more assertive when it comes to sex. A man wants his wife to embrace her sexuality and be actively interested in sex and her own pleasure. This is his ultimate aphrodisiac.

Ladies, are you willing to take charge and be in control of your desires? Do you want to feel confident in your sensual power? Do you have desires for erotic power, but resist because that's not what "good girls" do?

The media would have you believe that dominant women are angry, leather-clad dominatrices. The truth is that the real, sexually dominant woman lives among us, and she is no stereotype. She might be the young intern at your office or a member of your school's PTA or she might be the sweet old lady on the bus.

It's easy to find famous icons of sexy and empowered women, but we easily ignore the power of the strong, sexy feminine in the everyday woman. You don't have to be a Hollywood starlet to be strong, sexy, and feminine. It doesn't take fame, fortune, or personal trainers to be sexy. Every woman has the potential to be sexy; some just don't know how to find that hidden potential, and others intentionally bury it.

So what is the secret to being sexy? It's actually quite simple: confidence. A woman who carries herself with confidence and faces the challenges of an ordinary life with grace and determination is inherently sexy. Unfortunately, there is no step-by-step guide to achieving this confidence. It is something each woman must discover for herself. However, once you find this self-confidence, no one and nothing can take it from you. Once you have it, it doesn't matter how old you are, what you're wearing, or what you're doing—you can always be a confident, strong, sensual, sexy woman.

Embracing the Sexually Empowered Woman

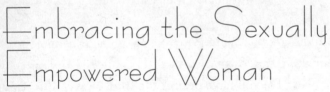

What deeply arouses your partner isn't a long list of sexual activities that may intrigue him. While those activities are enjoyable, they're nothing without your delivery. It's about your attitude! If your husband senses that your heart isn't in it, it kills the thrill. He'll likely go along with it just to have a curiosity satisfied. He may even show that he appreciates the act that he knows you are grudgingly giving him. You can see how this can create ugly resentments and a vicious cycle of destructive non-communication. So keep it real. Feel confident and empowered enough in your own sexuality to speak your mind and tell him what *you want*.

In the same way that you define your feminine self, he may have a list of attributes that he'd like to see in you. Although not all men have consciously thought about this, all men are aware of female qualities that appeal to them, no matter how committed they are to you. Find out what dominant attributes appeal to him. Then find ways to match your styles of dominance, and you have the golden key to inspiring unparalleled joy in your partner. Add the physically delightful play that you'll discover later in the book, and you will have just created magic for the both of you.

Some of your partner's favorite power-femme characteristics may not match yours. Don't force them to match or try to act like something you're not. For example, you'll never find "ice queen" on my list; I'm just too chipper for that. If I attempted to be an ice queen, it would feel stiff, staged, and boring. But if my husband said that he'd like it if I were "witty," "creative," or "dominating," I could do those!

Don't hesitate to try on a new style or attribute. If it feels good, keep it. If it doesn't fit, drop it and move on. Whatever you do should please you. In addition to being a virtue in its own right, pleasing yourself is also the best way of pleasing your man.

Now that you've discovered a little more about your personal sexual core, let's talk about what makes for an empowered woman of quality.

Confidence: The Root of Power

Never forget that the ultimate aphrodisiac is genuine self-confidence. Some people may challenge this because cockiness often comes off as abrasive. The difference between cockiness and self-confidence is the source of validation. The cocky woman needs to see her greatness reflected in the eyes of others, while the confident woman knows that her power source is from within. She has taken inventory of and is comfortable with her own talents, skills, assets, and strengths. She is confident enough to see her own flaws clearly. The confident woman is defined by a sense of self and comfort in her own identity as erotically dominant.

A Few Practical Tips

Now that we've discussed the philosophy of female sexual power, here are a few basic tips to help you begin creating a fulfilling sexual experience as a sexy, dominant woman:

† Once you've discussed this with your partner, put your satisfaction first. Focus on the activities on their wish list that will give *you* pleasure.

† Focus on enjoying one or two simple activities thoroughly, even if your partner's wish list is as long as your arm. It's better to do a few things well than many things poorly. If you leave him wanting more, that's a good thing.

- † Whenever you feel uncertain, take a slow breath and ask yourself, "What would please me right now?" Then follow through with what would please you.
- † Engage power-femme posture! Stand up straight, hold your head high, roll your shoulders back, lift your chest, and pull your navel in. Try this, and feel how it affects your sense of confidence.
- † Have fun! Whether your style is sweet and nurturing, fierce and demanding, or anything in between, remember that this is always about pleasure.

Being Sexy: A Man's Guide

Okay, guys, I'm finally done talking to the women. Welcome back. So what should men do to be sexier? The first thing to do is read everything I wrote above that was directed to the women, but just reverse the gender roles. No, I'm not saying that you should discuss which shade of lipstick looks best on you, but you should be just as willing and able to make similar necessary changes in your comportment and attitude. What's good for the goose is good for the gander. So guys, pause here now and go back to the beginning of this chapter to see what I told the ladies and how you can apply those messages to you. I'll wait here.

Now that you've done that, I'm going to add a few things that are more gentleman-specific. First, be appreciative. If she's making an effort, even if it doesn't achieve the immediate and complete results you want, you must express gratitude. In the first section for the women above, I harped on how important a sexy attitude is. For you men, a kind and gracious attitude is even more of a turn-on for her than your hot butt in a pair of tight jeans.

I reminded the women that you like them to look nice; now I'm going to remind you that they like you to *be* nice. Seducing a woman takes words, not necessarily rock-hard abs. If your wife tries to show you her newfound sexiness and you brush her off or criticize her, you can rest assured that she'll be back in the flannel nighties in no time. So be nice!

Second, be romantic. For women, romance is a necessary prerequisite to sex. Romance shows your wife that you care about her, that she's special to you. Regular romance can do a lot to remind her why she's glad to be married to you. And when she's glad to be married to you, she'll remind you of why you're glad to be married to her.

If you're worried about romance breaking the bank, not every romantic gesture has to involve expensive dinners or jewelry. Creativity always counts more than cost. You can be just as romantic by playing the song that you first danced to, or by writing her a love poem. If you show your wife that she's worthy of being seduced, then she'll act as though she's worthy of being seduced.

Genital Esteem

As common as body dissatisfaction is, I think that genital dissatisfaction may be even higher. There are so many people out there who dislike the way that their genitals look, feel, or smell. A lot of men think that their penises aren't big enough or are too curved or that their scrotum hangs too low. A lot of women don't think that their vulvas are "feminine" enough (although it's a *vulva*—by definition, it's one of the most feminine things on the planet!). But if you're not comfortable with your genitals, it can be nearly impossible for you to feel sexy, especially when your partner is undressing you.

To a certain extent, our society's obsession with sex and the proliferation of pornography have exacerbated this problem. In porn, we're often presented with genitals that conform to an artificial standard of beauty. The women have vulvas that often have been operated on and computer enhanced until they merely appear as a single, hairless crack. The men in porn are often selected simply because they have unnaturally large penises, and then they are filmed at angles that exaggerate their size. No wonder some people don't feel like they measure up.

In some ways, our conservative culture's general emphasis on modesty actually doesn't help things, because it means that most of the time when we actually see someone nude, they've been specially picked, posed, lit, and airbrushed. As such, most Americans don't have a very good concept of what the "normal" human body looks like, whether male or female.

As with body image, genital esteem can also be improved through affirmations that specifically deal with the genitals. If people are comfortable with it, seeing depictions of real people who are naked (but without all of the careful primping, propping, and setup that you get with most photo shoots) can also help. There is a growing movement toward portraying average people and their genitals in all their diversity, normality, and glory. Jamie McCartney's sculpture "The

Great Wall of Vagina" features casts of 400 different women's vulvas, and it shows the wonderful diversity of appearance and form in female genitalia. Projects like "101 Penis" and "101 Vagina" by Philip Werner demonstrate in photographs how real people look when they are nude.

However you choose to do it, please try to come to peace with your genitals. Take my word for it. You're beautiful. You're amazing. And once you let yourself see it, you'll be so glad that you did. You'll find that you and your partner can connect in ways you never dreamed of when you finally start to love yourself.

Exercise: Being Sexy

Step 1: Closet Culling

This exercise works well if the two of you can do it together, but can work almost as well if just one of you is doing it at a time. Go into your closet and stare at your clothes; start pulling things off hangers. If you're doing this together, work on your own clothes, not your spouse's. Don't start making comments on what is not being pulled down. Just start getting rid of things that you know aren't attractive.

If you see your spouse getting rid of something that you think is sexy, it's okay to kindly say so. If your relationship is strong enough to take it, I invite you to ask your spouse if you should keep or discard a specific item of clothing. Having a conversation while you both do this will give each of you insight into what looks sexy to your spouse and what doesn't.

Your goal is to end up with just two comfy outfits, and the rest are sexy outfits. If that means you end up with only two outfits in your closet and a pile of everything else, so be it. But this needs to be *your* goal regarding *your* clothes. If your spouse takes over and starts tossing things, you're going to resent it and just refill your closet with the same kinds of clothes.

Step 2: Replenishing

Get a couple of fashion magazines, both for men and women. Guys, hand the male magazine to her, and you take the female magazine. Take a high-lighter and go through it marking things you like. (Ladies, don't just circle the washboard abs. You can't expect miracles this soon.) When you're done, trade magazines and see what your spouse marked and talk about it. Now that each of you has an idea of what your partner might like in your appearance, it's time for a little shopping.

Chapter 6

Scheduling Sex

When was the last time you had great sex? And I mean real, luxurious, intimate sex, not just the kind that you get over in a hurry so that you can get to sleep or so that you can get back to your favorite show or because the kids are going to be home in 15 minutes. I'm talking about the kind of sex that curls your toes from a stream of relentless orgasms, the kind of sex that makes you forget about the weight of the world on your shoulders and leaves you feeling completely satiated.

You might be saying, "Sounds great, but who has time for that kind of sex?" My simple answer is: "The couples who make time for it."

When couples first become sexually intimate, finding time for sex never seems to be a problem. The lawn may need to be mowed, the dishes may be piling up, and it may be 1:30 a.m. with work the next morning, but the sex will happen!

As you get further into a relationship, that often changes. You have children, a mortgage, demanding jobs, church obligations, pets, and many other things that need to be taken care of. You become busy, and sex gets pushed to the back burner. You then let sex happen when everything else is taken care of. You tell yourselves that sex can take place any time that you're not busy with other responsibilities. Unfortunately, because great sex can happen anytime, it soon starts happening at no time.

Admittedly, sometimes sex has to take a backseat. After all, we wouldn't accomplish much if we always walked around in a perpetual horny haze and did nothing but have sex. Parents need to care of their children; they need to work to support their families. But nonetheless, if we want to have a marriage that lasts and that leaves us feeling fulfilled, we need to find a way to confront the problem of being too busy for intimacy. We need to not see romance and sex as luxury items in our marriage, but as its lifeblood and vitality.

If you want to have great sex (and the fact that you're reading this book suggests that you do), you need to schedule it. This is one of the single most important pieces of counsel I have, and that's why, no matter what a couple's complaints are when they enter my office, one bit of advice I almost invariably give is to sit down together and schedule at least one time a week that will be their intimacy time.

When I suggest this, I often get a strange look and an incredulous reply that runs something like this: "Schedule sex? But what about the spontaneity? That's what makes sex so great!"

To this, I respond, "And how is spontaneity working for the two of you now?" Insanity is to do the same thing over and over and expect different results. If you want your sex life to be better, you're going to have to make some changes.

And scheduling time for sex is one of the best changes that you could possibly make.

There are many things that get in our way of having spontaneous sex, but by scheduling it, you can make sex the priority that it should be. For example, at the end of the day, it's hard to give your spouse spontaneous attention after having spent all day working, taking care of kids, running errands, cleaning the house, and so on. In situations like this, a lot of couples end up either just not having sex or having perfunctory, sleepy quickies. Neither one is a good solution for keeping the spark in your marriage.

However, if you can make the leap to scheduling intimate time on a Friday night or Saturday afternoon, then you can have sex when both of you are awake and have the time to really explore and celebrate.

Scheduled time for intimacy allows for better preparation. Some people have a hard time letting go and enjoying sex when the house is messy or the dishes aren't done. By scheduling sex, you can both do some chores in advance of your appointment.

Scheduling time for sex also allows for personal preparation. Sex is usually more pleasant when you're both groomed, clean, and smell nice.

As important as physical preparation is, mental preparation is also important. Do you remember when you were dating and you found yourself daydreaming and looking forward to the next time that you would see each other? The anticipation that comes from scheduling sex can allow you to recapture those feelings. Anticipation isn't merely fun; the preparation time can give you time to switch out of "businesswoman" or "mommy" mode and into "sexy seductress."

Having time to anticipate and prepare mentally can help with these transitions.

Just because the sex is scheduled doesn't mean that there can't be surprises. These can be the fun undies you're wearing or the texts you send leading up to your date. The spontaneity may be in deciding to make love on the living room couch or kitchen table because you've planned ahead and gotten all of the kids out of the house. In some cases, scheduling sex makes greater variety and experimentation possible precisely because it is planned out ahead of time. It's scheduled spontaneity!

Scheduling sex may lead to other benefits as well. Some couples find that it's actually easier to cuddle, kiss, and fondle during their "days off," because they both know that it won't lead to sex. The husband knows not to get frustrated from the lack of sexual release. The wife knows that the touch is genuine closeness and not a disguised sexual overture. This understanding lets the couple cuddle and be close without the potential for suspicion, games, or hurt feelings.

One couple that tried this exercise told me that on the nights they scheduled sex they were "both more into it and the sex has been great." Another said, "We went from spending most nights keeping pillows between us on the bed to spooning." These responses are not unique. Just about every couple who has tried this exercise has found that it makes their sex sexier, more intimate, and much more fun.

And you know what? All the couples also report that they've had sex—spontaneously—on other days, too. Scheduling sex may actually be the single best thing that you can do for your levels of spontaneous sex. So grab your partner and your calendars and schedule away.

Some of you women may be wondering what to do if you arrive at your appointment and you're just not in the mood. Should you reschedule? In general, I'd say no. I'd really encourage you to still make your sex appointment happen. Recent research indicates that women (more likely than men) can feel desire *as a result* of physical stimulation. I know this sounds pushy, but in some cases, I encourage women to start the act and then see if desire doesn't follow.

So even if you're not in the mood, if you're willing to try, I'd advise you to just press on and see if things take off. When doing this, it's fine to be honest with your spouse and let him know that you're willing to move ahead and see how things go.

Dating Your Spouse

Connected to the idea of scheduling sex is the idea of scheduling time for other types of intimacy. I am a huge fan of couples having a regular date night. Sometimes this may coincide with your scheduled sex, sometimes it may not. However, I believe that couples should set aside time each week to just be a couple. Couples work so hard on so many things. They have to worry about making their job schedules line up, about paying bills and filing insurance claims, about repairing the car and house, about making sure their children are fed and clothed and played with—the list goes on and on! No wonder married couples sometimes feel more like siblings, roommates, or coworkers than like lovers.

Your date night is a time for you to focus on your relationship as a couple, as lovers. It will help you to rediscover what it is that you love about each other and why you fell in love in the first place. Trust me, it's worth it.

Exercise: Scheduling Sex

Find a time when the two of you can be alone.
Get your calendars out and decide what times
you would like to schedule sex. I'd like for you to
schedule intimacy at least once a week. However, if
you'd like, you can certainly feel free to schedule it
more frequently. Take into account all of the factors
that you can think of. Think about where your kids
will be. Think about when the big projects are due
at work. Think about the piano recitals and swim-
ming lessons and baseball games.

Pick times that will give the best setting for sex,
and remember to give yourself a good, long chunk
of time. A lot of the best sex happens when you're
not rushing to a goal and when you can luxuriate.

When you've picked the times for sex, write
them in your calendar. If you're too embarrassed to
actually write "SEX" in your calendar, you can use
a code word. However, there's something to be said
for being bold. Seeing "SEX" in your calendar will
make you smile, and it will remind you that sex is
nothing to be ashamed of. Once you've written it
down, it's an appointment, and treat it as seriously
as you would a work commitment. Your marriage is
worth prioritizing, and treating your scheduled time

as sacred tells your spouse that you love and value him or her as much as anything else in your life.

To see how scheduled sex can benefit you, I'd like you to schedule sex for one month. At the end of that month, evaluate what positive things this exercise has brought into your sex life; then you can decide if you'd like to continue to make it a part of your routine.

Part II

The first section helped you understand intimacy and desire and gave you permission to pursue them. It taught you to talk openly with your spouse and reminded you of what it means to be sexy. It also encouraged you to ensure that you make time for sex.

This next section will help you know what to do once you lock the bedroom door.

Chapter 7

Relax, Just Do It

Although *relaxation* doesn't sound terribly sexy, it is crucial for good sex. Stress and tension activate the sympathetic nervous system, which is responsible for the fight-or-flight response, as opposed to the parasympathetic nervous system, which is critical for arousal.

These two nervous systems (sympathetic and parasympathetic) battle each other and keep each other in check, which means that stress and tension can short-circuit the arousal process. Many women find that relaxation is necessary before they can even think about sex. Stress can also have a negative effect on a man's sexual response. Erection is controlled by the parasympathetic nervous system, which means that men who have erectile challenges may need to learn to relax.

We all carry tension in our minds and bodies, and sometimes we get so used to carrying it around that we don't even realize it's there anymore. The following exercises let you recognize and release the tension you are carrying, so if you're feeling tense before sex, take ten minutes for one of these exercises. Also, if you perform these exercises on a regular basis, you can train your body and mind to relearn the difference between tense and relaxed. If you are consistent in your practice, you'll find that you have an easier time controlling your thoughts, remaining calm, and getting into the mood.

Perform the first exercise before moving on to the second. The strong feelings of tension in the first exercise are easier to distinguish than the light, barely perceptible feelings in the second.

Exercise: Progressive Muscle Relaxation

Progressive Muscle Relaxation 1

Find a place where you won't be interrupted. Loosen your clothing and get comfortable. Either lie down or sit in a position where your back and neck are well supported.

Close your eyes and take five deep breaths in and out. Focus on your breathing and let all thoughts leave your mind.

Strongly tighten the muscles in your toes, while leaving all other muscles in your body loose and relaxed and breathing deeply and slowly. Note what the tension feels like, and hold it for a count of ten. Relax and enjoy the sensation of release from tension.

Then, flex the muscles in your feet. Again, hold for a count of ten. Relax.

Slowly move up your body, from muscle group to muscle group, alternately tensing and relaxing the muscles in the following order: calves, thighs, buttocks, pelvic floor, abdomen, lower back, chest, upper back, shoulders, and neck. Finally, tense and relax your facial muscles.

Take five more deep breaths in and out, enjoying the sensation of a body that is relaxed. When you are ready, open your eyes.

Progressive Muscle Relaxation 2

Just as in the last exercise, get into a comfortable position and close your eyes. Take five deep breaths, letting all your thoughts drift away as you focus on your breathing.

Slightly tighten your right hand so that you feel only the smallest amount of tension. Hold it at this level. Be sure that you continue to breathe, and be sure that you're not tensing any other part of your body.

After holding the slight tension for several seconds, let the tension go, allowing your right hand to relax completely. Note how your hand feels different now than it did a few seconds ago while you had it tensed. Observe any difference in feelings between your right and left hands. Is your right hand more relaxed than your left?

Now tense your left hand, again only going to the point where you can first start to feel the tension. Feel the tightness, then release it, feeling the relaxation spread through the rest of your body.

Continue this process throughout the rest of your body. Tense your right forearm slightly, then your left. Then tense and relax your right and left upper arms. Then tense your shoulders slightly, raising them almost imperceptibly toward your ears. As you do this, make sure your neck stays loose. Notice the tension in your shoulders and how it makes them feel different from the rest of your body.

Tense your neck, then let it go. Do the same with your facial muscles, then your scalp. Make sure your whole head is loose and relaxed. Your jaw should be slack. Your eyes should be relaxed, motionless, and rolled back in their sockets, and the muscles around them should feel heavy and still. Your tongue should lie gently at the base of your mouth. Make sure your forehead is smooth and still.

Now, tense your right and left pectoral muscles, and let them relax. Then tense your back muscles, arching imperceptibly against the bed or chair. Then relax again. Tense your stomach. Keep breathing as you let it go and relax.

Tighten your right, then your left buttock. Tighten your pelvic floor, then let it go, allowing a feeling of openness in your groin.

Tense your right thigh, then your left thigh. Tense your right, then your left calf. Tighten your feet, and then your toes. With each muscle group you tense and relax, let yourself reach an even deeper level of relaxation, calmness, and serenity.

Take another few deep breaths. Then minimally tense every muscle in your body at the same time. Again, only tighten the muscles to the point where you feel the slightest tension. You should feel this tension throughout your whole body. Notice the sensation as you keep breathing. Then let your whole body relax. Feel a wave of calmness and relaxation wash over you as you release the tension from your muscles.

Breathe deeply, enjoying the feeling of relaxation. Really try to internalize how it feels to be completely relaxed. When you're ready, gradually begin to move your fingers and toes, then stretch. When you're ready to return to your day, slowly open your eyes.

Sensual Touch

One could argue that we live in an overly *sexualized* world, but no one can claim that we live in an overly sensual world. How often do we linger over our food and really enjoy it instead of picking it up at a drive-through and downing it before we get home? How often do we just sit outside and feel the grass under our feet, the wind in our hair, and the sun against our skin?

Sensuality, as I use the term, means being connected to our five senses. It means being in the here and now, totally rooted into our body. It means totally feeling the sexual experience. It is the antithesis of, as the saying goes, "just lying back and thinking of England," or of our grocery list, or if this position makes my breasts look saggy.

Understanding the mind-body connection is an absolute necessity for good sex, and I'll share a secret with you: when you're living sensually, enjoying all of the unique feelings that come in through your senses, you don't get bored, even when you do the same thing repeatedly. It's when we get into our analytical, critical side that we start overthinking things and get bored with repetitive experiences.

Sex is one repetitive experience that we find ourselves drawn to again and again. If we're not careful, this familiarity can turn to tedium. But no matter how many times we've had sex, a sensual approach can give life and vibrancy to our intimacy. Sex can become a sort of sacrament, a ritual experience where we come together and do similar things, but with ever-increasing meaning and value.

The following sensual touch exercises will help you and your partner cultivate sensuality and connect through touch. When couples who are having sexual difficulties come to me, depending on the situation, I may recommend that they refrain from sexual intercourse and orgasm for a period of time (anywhere from a week to a month, depending on the couple) and perform these exercises. This can reduce anxiety and feelings of expectations, because neither partner needs to perform. There is no pressure to have an erection or achieve orgasm. There is no goal except to enjoy sensation, so there is little possibility for failure.

Even couples that don't want to abstain from sex can benefit from these sensual exercises. However, don't allow this exercise to lead to sex, as this would cloud the expectations and results of the experience.

Decide how long you will avoid intercourse and orgasm as you do these exercises, making sure that you take both partners' desires into account. Ideally, you should plan on dedicating at least a week for each exercise, and you should also plan on performing each exercise at least a few times.

Fair Fighting Rules

I interject these basic rules for conflict management here because it's possible that as you start to do these hands-on exercises, you may encounter a little strife between the two of you. I hope that's not the case, but if you do run into arguments, I want you to be prepared on how to best deal with them.

Life would be calmer if we could avoid all conflict. However, avoiding arguments isn't necessarily beneficial to long-term marital happiness. Couples who avoid conflict are actually *less* satisfied in their relationships than couples that allow disagreements. In marriage, the usual ratio of positive to negative interactions is about five to one, which means that if you prohibit any conflict, you may actually miss out on a lot of positive experiences.

The lists below are simple and fairly obvious. The real challenge comes in obeying the rules, even when your partner won't. Don't expect that either of you will be perfect "fighters" every time. But as you do have conflicts, look back at this list and see where you may have slipped. After things have simmered down, calmly discuss what you did well and what needs improvement.

DO:

† Prepare for difficult conversations. Organize your thoughts and feelings before talking. This will help you know what you want to say, and it may reduce your anxiety.

† Choose your purpose. Not all problems need to be solved right away. Sometimes you just need to discuss what happened and find out how everyone is feeling.

† Embrace curiosity. Instead of assuming you know how your partner feels and why they interpreted a situation a certain way, find out from *them* how they feel and why.

† Realize that your partner may see things differently. We all have different histories and experiences, and these affect the way we approach decisions. Because we come into situations with different attitudes and different amounts of information, we necessarily perceive things differently.

† Share your purpose. If you just need someone to listen, let your partner know. On the other hand, if a problem really needs solving, make that clear, too.

† Be accountable. Take responsibility for your part in the problem.

† Search for common ground, not disagreement. Use "and" statements, not "but" statements.

† Listen and be open to persuasion. See if you can figure out why you and your partner see the issue so differently. Based on what you learn, consider changing the way you understand the situation.

† Seek to share information, not to win an argument. Rather than trying to convince your partner to take your side, approach the conversation from the perspective of sharing information.

† Know when to use humor. Humor can be very helpful, especially when it's self-deprecating. Gentle

humor can help you both to keep perspective and stay engaged in the conversation.

† Remember the love you share.

DON'T:

† Don't hit and run. Don't start a potentially problematic conversation with an offhanded comment on your way out the door. Find a time when you can actually have your conversation.

† Don't try to persuade. Try to understand the other person's point of view, rather than aiming to change their perspective.

† Don't disregard the other person's perspective. If you've only come prepared to share *your* solution or answer to a problem, you're in for big trouble.

† Don't use humor as a weapon. Beware of jokes or sarcasm that are mean-spirited.

† Don't resort to name-calling or character judgments.

† Don't bring up past issues. Once an issue is resolved, don't bring it up in the next fight. Bringing up a past failure to make a point in the present is a horrible idea.

† Don't place blame. Assigning blame is the quickest route to defensiveness and denial.

† Don't let your nonverbal signals override your words. Sometimes gestures, such as eye-rolling, can have a bigger impact on the conversation than what you actually say.

† Don't use words like "always" and "never."

† Don't push for a particular outcome.

† Don't take it personally.

† Don't argue for the sake of arguing.

† Don't play games.

† Don't ever use sex as a weapon, a tool, or a reward.

Exercise: Just Touch

A bit of background information before you begin: Increasing libido means creating a sense of yearning and anticipation before and during sexual activity. However, rushed movements give no chance for desire or anticipation to build, and may instead trigger feelings of annoyance.

Also, the body can become overstimulated by intense, rapid movement. Slowing down the movements gives the opportunity to mentally anticipate the next wave of pleasure. This exercise will help you slow down while heightening anticipation of touch and bringing your partner to higher levels of sensory awareness and pleasure.

Although arousal is not the goal of this exercise, there is nothing wrong with feeling aroused during it. Simply enjoy and notice whatever feelings and sensations you have without judging or trying to control them. Now for the exercise:

§ Both of you take off your clothes and lie down together somewhere comfortable.

§ Ask your partner to lie down, close his or her eyes, breathe deeply, and relax.

- Ask your partner to try to anticipate where you are going to touch him or her next as you do this exercise.
- Begin by holding your hands just above your partner's skin for a minute. Hold them close enough to allow him or her to sense the heat from your hands.
- Place your hands slowly and gently down on the same spot.
- Slowly lift them and pick a nearby area. Again, hold your hand just above the skin for a minute before actually putting it down.
- Slowly perform this same action all over your partner's body.
- Lie down and relax while your partner performs the same exercise on you.

Variation

If you desire, you can also use parts of your body other than your hands to touch your partner. Each part of the body registers touch in a slightly different way. Notice how different it feels for both you and your partner when you use different parts of your body.

Follow-up

After you have finished, talk with your partner about your experience of touching and being touched. Discuss any emotions you may have experienced, whether positive or negative. What did you like about this? What did you dislike? Are there aspects of this sort of touch that you would like to incorporate into your life or your lovemaking?

Exercise: Sensual Touch

In this exercise, you will be touching parts of the body other than the common erogenous zones, including the face, feet, and hands. The purpose of this exercise is not to create arousal, but to simply create intimacy between you and your spouse without any further expectations.

Preparation

- As you plan for this exercise, decide where and when you'll do it, and schedule a sufficient block of time to allow you to be unhurried as you enjoy yourselves and each other.
- You may want to use a massage oil or lubrication to help reduce friction as you touch your partner. Olive oil, silicone lube, and coconut oil are excellent for this sort of touch.

Sensual Touch

- One partner lies face down while the other partner caresses them as gently and tenderly as possible.

§ If you are the giver, start with the back of the head, the ears, and the neck. Then move down the back and the sides to the buttocks and the insides of the thighs. From there, move gently to the legs and the feet.

§ If you are the receiver, focus on the sensation of being touched and the feelings it brings up. Stay in the moment and in your body, not your thoughts. If outside thoughts intrude, don't judge them or worry; just acknowledge them and let them go. Feel free to give verbal feedback to the giver. Let them know what feels good. Also let them know if anything feels unpleasant, being as specific as possible (i.e., if it's too fast or too slow, too hard or too soft).

§ The giver should also focus on his or her own sensations. What does the skin feel like under his or her hands? What speed and pressure of caress feels best to give? The giver should let intrusive thoughts slip away and just focus on the sensation of touching.

§ Once the giver has enjoyed touching the posterior side of the body, he or she should signal the receiver to turn over.

§ Caress the front of the body in the same way. Start with the head and face, caress the chest, belly and sides, legs and feet. However, avoid touching the genitals and nipples.

§ Arousal is not the purpose of this exercise, but there's nothing wrong with arousal either. The receiver should enjoy whatever sensations and feelings come, without judging them, whether they're sexual or not.

§ Continue this exercise until the receiver has had enough, but make sure that you save enough time for both partners to experience each role.

§ If, during this exercise, one of you develops excessive anxiety, feel free to discontinue.

§ Once you're done, trade places and repeat.

Exercise: Caressing

These caressing exercises are similar to the Sensual Touch exercise (page 96). For people who found too many roadblocks to perform Sensual Touch, these can provide a more limited and controlled way to experience touch. Because they are narrow in scope, they can also sometimes provide a more focused, deeper feeling of intimacy. As such, they can also be used as a supplemental act before moving on to Arousing Touch on page 107.

Guidelines

§ Just as with all of these exercises, find a time and place where the two of you won't be disturbed. Decide who will begin as giver and who will begin as receiver. Halfway through the session, you will switch so that you both get a chance to fill each role.

§ Let the receiver choose the part of the body to be caressed: hands, face, or feet. (See individual exercises below).

§ Keep in mind that these exercises require a light touch—caressing, not massage. As opposed to massage, which is meant to loosen the muscles, light stroking activates the nerves only, and it can produce a wonderful richness of sensation. Light caresses can also feel particularly gentle and tender.

§ Maintain body contact throughout the exercise. When contact is broken, it is easy for the receiver to grow ticklish or lose concentration.

§ Ticklishness may be a manifestation of the receiver disconnecting from the body, or it may be the psyche's defense against the potential source of sensual pleasure. Feeling ticklish obstructs being touched and inhibits sensations that might otherwise be sexual. If you as the receiver start to feel ticklish, try to relax and focus on sensation; the giver should temporarily use a slightly firmer touch.

Face Caress

§ Prior to beginning the facial caress, the receiver should remove any makeup.

§ The giver sits in a manner that provides good back support and places a pillow in his lap. The receiver lies down, places her head on the pillow, and closes her eyes. (Note: If you are using lotion, be very cautious around the eyes.)

§ Begin by cradling the face between your hands. Then glide your hands slowly upward through the hair and over the scalp.

§ Move to the forehead and, using your thumbs or fingers, stroke from the center toward the temples. Repeat several times.

§ Moving downward, stroke the eyebrows. Then delicately caress the lids and eyelashes. Repeat several times.

§ Continue down the face to the nose and cheeks. Use your thumbs to stroke downward on the side of the nose and then downward just under the cheekbones.

§ Glide your fingers upward through the hair before returning your thumbs to the nose.

§ Make gentle, circular motions on the cheeks with your fingertips. Experiment with performing the same stroke with the palms of your hands.

§ As you move toward the mouth, stroke the area above the lips. Then trace around the edges of the lips with your fingertips. Finally, caress the lips themselves.

§ As you proceed to the chin, try feathery downward strokes while moving along the jawline.

§ Move to the neck. Here, use gentle upward strokes.

- ⚶ Proceed to the ears. Use your fingers and thumbs to explore all over them, but do not probe inside.
- ⚶ Use both hands to carefully lift and turn the head, then let it rest on one side. Stroke the exposed side and back of the neck. Then turn the head to the other side and repeat.
- ⚶ Straighten out the head and run your hands through the hair. Then bring your hands to rest gently on the face for a minute before releasing them.
- ⚶ Share your feelings with your partner at the conclusion of the session.

Foot Caress

- ⚶ Be prepared to change position as often as needed to remain comfortable while performing the foot caress. When you change positions, make sure that you maintain body contact.
- ⚶ Begin by bathing your partner's feet. (If you have a religious background, you may notice the symbolism here.) Use one bucket or small tub for washing, another for rinsing.
- ⚶ Gently place one of your partner's feet into a tub of warm water. Slowly wash the foot with soap. Place your partner's other foot in the water as well and wash it.
- ⚶ After both feet have been washed, lift the first foot from the water and place it on a towel.

Re-lather the foot and then place it in a rinsing tub. Repeat this process for the other foot.

§ Remove each foot from the rinse water and wrap each foot completely in a dry towel.

§ Unwrap one foot, then slowly and thoroughly dry it all over, including between the toes. Repeat with the other foot.

§ Once the feet are completely dry, oil or powder them.

§ Next, place the heel of one foot on your thigh so you can easily touch both the top and bottom surfaces. Cradle the foot between your hands for a moment to warm it, then begin stroking.

§ Begin your stroke on the lower calf. Using both hands, caress the ankle and foot to relax it.

§ Then, stroke the foot in circular motions with your thumbs, beginning at the toes and moving to the heels. Repeat several times.

§ Using your thumb and finger, stroke each toe along its entire length. Run your pinky slowly between each toe.

§ Rub each of the toes, paying particular attention to the pad on the bottom of the big toe.

§ Experiment with different ways of caressing the foot. You can use one finger, the heel of your hands, or several fingers together.

§ Vary the speed of your stroking. If your partner doesn't become ticklish, try feathering strokes and use your fingernails.

§ Conclude by cupping the foot between your hands for a moment.

- Repeat with the other foot.
- Share your feelings with your partner at the conclusion of the session.

Hand Caress

- As with the foot caress, be prepared to change position as often as needed to remain comfortable while performing the hand caress. When you change positions, make sure that you maintain body contact.
- Get into a position that is comfortable for both partners. Throughout the caressing, the receiver should leave his hands limp and passive.
- Pick up one of your partner's hands, and do not let go until you are ready to move to the other hand.
- Both you and your partner should concentrate fully on the sensations in your hands and the feelings evoked by the sensations.
- Explore your partner's hand using all the different parts of your own hands. Lightly stroke the hand with your thumb and forefinger, making gentle circular missions. Then try using your palm, different parts of the fingers, and the back of your hands and see how the sensation differs.
- Notice the texture, the folds and shape of the whole hand: palm, fingers, nails. You may find that closing your eyes helps you both to focus on the sensations.

- When you have finished with one hand, hold it, palm downward, between your hands for a few moments before putting it down and moving to the other.
- Repeat on the other hand.
- Share your feelings with your partner at the conclusion of the session.

Kissing

The next subject is so dear to me that I'd like to write an entire book on nothing but this: kissing.

Lovers have been using kisses to express intimacy for a long time. There's something inherently intimate about kissing. The lips are rich with nerve endings, and the act of pressing and rubbing them against one's lover is both pleasurable and intimate. The act can almost overwhelm us with sensory input: sight, smell, touch, and taste are all involved in the perfect kiss.

Do you remember when you were first courting, how you ached to kiss each other? Kissing was bliss. Whether you merely exchanged chaste and quivering kisses or spent hours "making out," kissing was likely the highlight of your intimate time together. You looked forward to kissing before it happened, and then after the date was over, you went home and relived the experience again, thinking about the feeling of their lips on yours.

So, given that that's how you felt then, how do you feel about kissing now? Is kissing simply relegated to a formal peck on the way out the door? Are your kisses perfunctory and passionless? Do you still *feel* the sensation of kissing, or have you started just checking out and mechanically pressing lips to lips?

Kissing can be a good barometer for a relationship. If the passion is gone from your kissing, then some fire has likely gone from your marriage as well. Thankfully, the reverse is also true. If you can increase your intimacy and enjoyment in your kissing, you'll also reap rewards in your relationship.

Improving your kissing is easy. All it takes is to give yourself to the moment and to enjoy the sensations. It's when we take kissing for granted and check out that kissing grows boring. When we're firmly invested in our bodies, we can kiss for hours and never grow tired of it.

If you'd like to improve the passion in your kissing, you're ready to try the Kissing exercise.

Exercise: Kissing

This is simple and doesn't require much planning or warning. Just keep these next ideas in mind as you encounter your partner throughout the day.

Double kiss: The next time you kiss, bring your spouse back in for one more. This unexpected little addition will give them a bit more gleam in their eye.

Long kiss: Those extra moments will bring desire rushing into the moment; whether or not you can succumb to it at the time doesn't matter. Just enjoy those extra few seconds of kissing.

After you've started incorporating these two simple tips into your kissing for about a week, feel free to discuss the effects with your partner and see what it has done for your relationship.

Just like there are a multitude of sexual positions, there are limitless ways and places to kiss: butterfly kisses, open-mouth "French" kisses, massaging kisses, and kissing other parts of the body, even up to and including oral sex. (But that's a topic for another time.)

I know a couple that's been married for almost ten years that regularly incorporates this exercise as a part of their date nights. Because of their religious beliefs, they avoided passionate kissing and making out while they were courting. But now, they enjoy getting to do all the things they avoided prior to marriage. After dinner or a movie, they'll drive off to a deserted lovers' lane and just enjoy the simple joys of making out. And when they get home afterward, they say the sex is mind-blowing.

Now that you've completed a sensual touch or caressing exercise, and revisited the wonders of romantic kissing, how did it go? Discuss the experience with your spouse. If you didn't feel much, or if you found your mind wandering, don't despair or judge yourself. If you felt anxious or impatient during the exercise, consider why these feelings may have come up.

I encourage you to try it again; training yourself to focus on your body instead of your mind can take some practice.

This next exercise builds upon the basic touch exercises, but adds in arousal. It is designed to encourage you and your partner to savor each other sexually. The better the foundation of sensual experience that you gain in the first exercise, the more benefit and enjoyment you'll gain from the second.

When you're ready, try this exercise. And as you do it, remember: slower is better. Slowing down allows both of you to really enjoy the experience and to luxuriate in sensuousness.

Exercise: Arousing Touch

As with Sensual Touch, you will be touching various parts of the body in this exercise. However, this exercise will include touching the erogenous zones—genitals and nipples—with the purpose of arousal. Though this exercise is aimed at erection and engorgement of the genitals for both partners, the goal is not orgasm. Partners should focus only on arousing their spouse.

Preparation

§ I highly recommend you have some lube, especially when touching the genitals.

§ Throughout this exercise, pay attention to your feelings and sensations. If something feels exceptionally good or if something feels very unpleasant, say so. It's perfectly fine to give feedback. However, it's also great to just be still and quiet, letting your body tune in to the experience.

Arousing Touch

- Just as with the Sensual Touch exercise, one partner will be the giver and the other will be the receiver. Find a position that is comfortable for both partners.
- If time allows, go through the first Sensual Touch exercise (or an abbreviated version of it) to "tune in the body" and get both of you into a sensual mode.
- Once both of you are feeling sensually connected, begin to caress the body with the intent to arouse. Move from one part of the body to another, doing things that feel good to the receiver. Caress the face, the belly, the ears, the thighs. Don't just make a beeline for the erogenous zones. The whole body can be erotic. Give it its due. Do as much body caressing as desired to arouse your partner before moving to the chest and groin.
- While the giver is caressing, the receiver should simply lie there and receive the touch. Enjoy it, don't analyze it. Don't become lost in your thoughts; be an active recipient. Give yourself to the sensation. As you do this, let your whole body be loose and heavy. Even as arousal grows, lie still, and avoid bringing tension into your body.

Giving Arousing Touch to a Man

ᔈ When you're touching him, it is okay if he doesn't achieve an erection. The penis is very sensitive, and it can still feel pleasure even when it's flaccid. Whether his penis is erect or not, touch it gently and lightly, and move slowly. The goal is not for him to necessarily achieve an erection, but rather for you to provide the stimulation that *could* allow it.

ᔈ As you touch him, don't spend too much time on one area; be very soft and gentle and avoid repetitive motions. The purpose of this touch is arousal, not orgasm.

ᔈ Caress the penis for a while, then move to another part of the body for a while. Don't worry if his erection goes down. That is natural and normal. It's fine for the erection to come and go.

ᔈ Alternate between genital touch and whole-body touch. This will increase arousal and help him to learn to appreciate other erogenous zones and be aware of arousing sensations throughout his whole body.

Giving Arousing Touch to a Woman

ᔈ Just like when she is caressing you, move from one area to another and don't go so quickly to the genitals. Even after you get there, be sure to move to other areas for a while. Watch her face and body language for signs that she wants you to stay on one area for a little longer. When in doubt, move around.

- ❧ When you do get to her groin, avoid repetitive stroking of the clitoris and don't insert anything in the vagina. Avoid repetitive motions that are designed to achieve orgasm. Remember, orgasm isn't the goal. If it happens accidentally, it's not a failure, but avoid trying to give her one.

- ❧ Men often feel a temptation to be goal-oriented during this sort of exercise. You must let go of that urge. You're not trying to give your partner an orgasm or even to maximize her level of arousal. You're trying to enjoy touching her and to let her enjoy being touched. As you let go of your need for performance, you'll find that both of you enjoy the experience more. Her level of arousal will come and go throughout the exercise, and this is just fine.

Arousing Touch Discussion

- ❧ When you finish, talk with your partner about the experience. Were there any parts that you especially enjoyed receiving? Were there any parts that you especially enjoyed giving? Tell your partner at least one thing that you liked about touching his or her body, or one thing that you learned by being touched.

§ As before, if one of you experiences excessive anxiety or distress, discontinue the exercise. Think about why these emotions may have come up and address them.

Never close your lips to those whom you have already opened your heart.
—Charles Dickens

Chapter 9

Sexual Touch for Men

Now that you have experienced sensual touch and arousing touch, you're ready to experience sexual touch. You've learned that your hands are some of the greatest sexual tools you have. They're more dexterous than any other part of the body, they never have erection problems, and they never have a headache. Knowing the right things to do with your hands can turn you from a sexual handyman to a sexual master.

The following genital touch techniques can be integrated into intercourse or they can be performed on their own. There's no rule that says that every sexual encounter must involve intercourse. In these cases, one partner pleasuring the other manually can be a great way to provide enjoyment, closeness, and show love when intercourse is for some reason unfeasible.

To start with, I'll give some general principles regarding genital touch. After we cover some of the philosophy, we can get into the fun stuff.

First, be invested. Nothing can ruin the mood like having you or your partner emotionally checking out. If you're loving your partner with your hands, really put your mind on that. Just because your genitals aren't involved, it isn't an excuse to zone out or work on the next day's to-do list. You're handling your partner's most private parts, which is a privilege and a trust, so respect and honor them. Do everything to show that you're fully invested: make eye contact, talk lovingly, use both hands, take an active position rather than lying back, remove your own clothes to allow skin-on-skin contact.

Second, let your partner set the pace. When you start turning your partner on, you may want to give them a quick release. Really, though, what's going to send them into worlds of ecstasy and make them come back to you again and again is if you draw things out no faster than their body begs for it. So when things start to get really hot and heavy and your partner seems close to orgasm, slow down, switch strokes, or move to another part of the body for a moment (but never long enough to make them actually feel frustrated). By the end, they'll be begging you to let them come. When they finally do, you'll see stars in their eyes, and they'll say that it was one of the best times they've ever had. Trust me.

Third, practice makes perfect. To start out with, you might not feel like a genius when it comes to pleasuring your partner. And that's okay.

Do your best, enjoy yourself, and engage your partner in lots and lots of communication. If you can get your partner's feedback about what sends them through the roof and which things were just so-so, then with time you'll be an expert at pleasuring your partner. And that's the goal.

Male Sexual Anatomy

You may have a variety of names for it, and I invite you to use terms that both of you like, but for now, I'll call it a penis. Penises come in all shapes, and size has nothing to do with function. Typically, the smaller a penis is when it's relaxed, the more it will grow when erect. Larger penises don't usually grow as much (and some don't grow at all) when they become erect. Some penises are pretty much straight, some curve to the side, some curve up, and some curve down. All of this is completely normal.

Penis   The penis has two parts: the shaft and the glans (or head). The head of the penis is more sensitive than the shaft. Other notable landmarks include the corona (the circular rim that runs around the base of the glans) and the frenulum (the spot on the underside of the penis where the head attaches to the shaft). In most men, the frenulum is the most sensitive sweet spot on the penis. In uncircumcised men, the foreskin is a retractable layer of skin that partially covers the head. In circumcised men, the foreskin has been surgically removed, and the glans is always exposed.

Scrotum   The scrotum is the loose pouch of skin that contains the testicles (or "balls"), which are very sensitive to pressure, so be very gentle with them. It is natural for one testicle to hang lower than the other. When a man is cold, his scrotum shrinks and his testicles retract toward his body.

When he is warm, the scrotal skin relaxes, and the testicles hang lower.

Prostate The prostate is a gland about the size of a walnut that is located between the rectum and the base of the penis. It secretes a milky white fluid that nourishes sperm and contributes to semen. Unlike the other male sexual organs, the prostate cannot be seen externally. It can be stimulated indirectly through the perineum or directly through the rectum.

Perineum The male perineum is the area between the scrotum and the anus. During arousal, the perineum can become sensitive and very receptive to stimulation and pleasure. Massaging the perineum can indirectly stimulate the prostate, and it can also provide stimulation to the root of the penis.

PC Muscle Suspended from the pelvic bone is a sling of muscle called the pubococcygeus muscle (or "PC muscle"). Learning to control it can help men to develop ejaculatory control. Once a man locates his PC muscle, he can do exercises called Kegels (page 145) to strengthen and control it.

Anus Although it isn't usually thought of as a part of a man's sexual anatomy, the anus can be a site of great sexual pleasure, and many men enjoy anal play as part of their sexual repertoire. The anus also provides access to the prostate for massage and other stimulation.

Before going further, I suggest that both partners get to know the man's sexual anatomy. Try to locate each of the features listed above (except perhaps the prostate—that's up to him). Be aware that the parts on your man may not look exactly as they do in the illustrations.

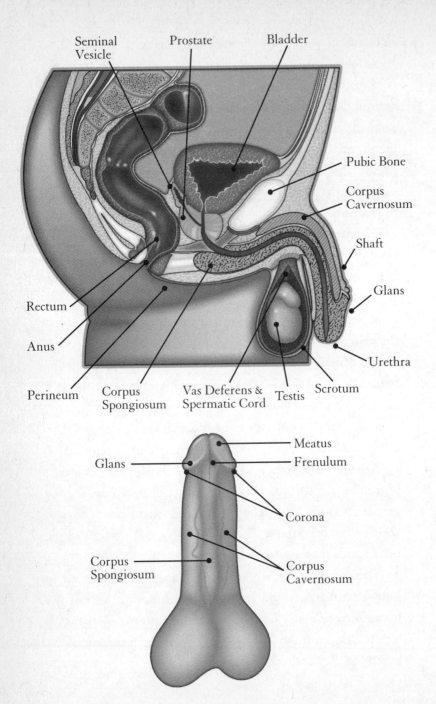

Seminal
Vesicle

Prostate

Bladder

Pubic Bone

Corpus
Cavernosum

Shaft

Glans

Urethra

Scrotum

Testis

Vas Deferens &
Spermatic Cord

Corpus
Spongiosum

Perineum

Anus

Rectum

Meatus

Frenulum

Glans

Corona

Corpus
Cavernosum

Corpus
Spongiosum

To Pleasure a Man

What's the best and easiest way for a woman to learn how to stimulate a man? Read his mind? Read a book? Ask a sexologist? No. The answer is obvious: have him tell you and have him show you. I'm not going to go into incredible detail on all the ways you can manually stimulate him. Those techniques are for another book.

You may be noticing that I'm not addressing whether or not it's okay for your husband to show you how he likes to be stimulated. You're right. I'm not addressing it. All I'm going to say is that not only do I think that it's okay, I think it's necessary. If you don't think it (or anything else I'm going to propose) is okay, then go back and read Chapter 2 and decide if you can press on. Now, back to the lesson.

As you try to replicate what he's taught you, pay attention to the grip strength, speed, amount of lube, variations, pauses, etc. When you do it, I encourage you to ask for feedback if you have any trouble reading his body language.

I said that I wouldn't give a comprehensive review of all the possible manual sexual techniques, but I will give a few options that the two of you can try. Some of these are the basic one-handed grip, the upside-down grip, and the okay-sign grip. In addition to the grips, there are an infinite variety of strokes, and I'm sure that if you look at other resources, you'll discover a multitude of colorful names for each of these, such as the traditional master stroke, the twister, the up-and-over, and the alternating fists, and they just get more elaborate from there. If you've made it this far in your experimentation with your partner, I hope that you're both communicating openly during these pleasuring sessions so that you can learn from him what works and what doesn't.

And don't take this all too seriously. This should be light-hearted fun. Feel free to laugh and giggle and be genuine with each other.

What to Do with a Flaccid Penis

Even in young and healthy men, it's very normal for a man's erection to wax and wane throughout a sexual encounter. This shouldn't worry you or him. Just think of it as giving you another way of stimulating him.

When he's soft, you may want to think less of stimulating it with the pumping action that we associate with sex. Instead, tease and caress it, gently stroking it with your fingers. You can touch his thighs and stomach and occasionally rub up against his penis. In fact, whether he's erect or not, massaging his stomach and chest with your hands while your forearm runs along his penis are quite erotic for a man.

There are also a number of techniques that can only be performed on a flaccid penis. Hold his penis at the base, and gently shake it back and forth or around in circles. This will give him a unique sensation, and it also encourages blood to flow into the penis.

Some men may also like it if you gently stretch their penis. Much like stretching the scrotum, you can grab the penis and pull it gently in different directions. Be gentle, and get feedback as to whether he likes it.

You can also try massaging or gently squeezing the penis. The flaccid penis is quite malleable, so you can use more pressure than you might with an erect penis. Massaging the penis may also help get the erectile tissue warmed up and ready to engorge. Try using a gentle, upward, milking stroke to see if he likes it.

You can also try rolling the penis between your hands, like you were trying to start a fire with two sticks. Place his penis between your palms, and then rub back and forth as if you were making a snake out of Play-Doh. As always, seek your partner's feedback with any technique you try.

Exercise: Give Him a Hand

- 𝆑 Find time when the two of you can be alone for a while.
- 𝆑 Let him know that you'd like to pleasure him with your hands.
- 𝆑 Don't set any other specific goals such as orgasm or intercourse, but if they happen naturally, it's fine.
- 𝆑 Both of you undress, and if you need some warm-up, consider starting with one of the exercises from earlier in the book.
- 𝆑 Lubricate your hands and, when he's ready, move to his penis.
- 𝆑 Practice a variety of techniques, with variations in tempo, pressure, and position. Make note of what he seems to like best and why.

§ Stroke your husband for as long as you both would like.

§ When you finish, snuggle and talk about the experience. Make note of techniques you would like to try again.

Chapter 10

Sexual Touch for Women

There's a lot of talk about how difficult men find it to make a woman orgasm, or how hard it can be for women to be "turned on" when their partner is craving quick sex. Yet men should take great pride in being able to pleasure a woman sexually because of the lore surrounding the elusive female orgasm.

However, if a man can master sexual touch on his partner, he can learn to pleasure a woman to the point of orgasm with his hands alone. Before reading further into these techniques and exercise, be sure to refer back to the introduction to Chapter 9, as the same general principles outlined there apply to sexual touch for women as well.

To Pleasure a Woman

Writing a chapter on how to pleasure women is difficult. It's a little bit like walking into a music store and asking if they can teach you how to play musical instruments. The only possible response to this question is another question: "Which instrument?" Casanova myths to the contrary, all women are different, and all women's desires are different. When it comes to sexual touch, some women love a light touch and some women love heavy stimulation. Some women love caressing directly on the clitoris, and some think that it's merely painful.

I've done my best to compile a list of good techniques that you can try, but it may take a lot of experimentation to figure out the best way to pleasure your woman in particular. The good news is that I don't think either of you will mind the practice very much.

This chapter focuses primarily on stimulation of a woman's external genitals. Although clitoral stimulation is not the only way for women to experience orgasm, it is the most common, and for many women it is the easiest way to climax. For information on the G-spot and other forms of stimulation, please visit the chapter entitled "Orgasmic Mastery for Women" on page 165.

Of course, before we can know how to stimulate the clitoris, we need to know what it is, where it is, and all of the fun things that surround it. So without further ado, let's talk a little about anatomy.

Female Sexual Anatomy

Although all women have pretty much the same parts as each other, there is vast diversity in the appearance and function of their genitals. The female genitals, inside and out, can look and operate very differently from one woman to the next, and they can even vary greatly in the same woman over time. Your body may look and work quite a bit differently from the examples shown here, and there is nothing wrong with that. Every vulva is beautiful and every vagina is wonderful.

Vulva   The vulva is a collective word that refers to all of a woman's external genitalia. People often mistakenly use the word "vagina" when speaking of a woman's visible genitalia, but this usage is technically incorrect.

Mons Pubis   The mons pubis is the large, padded area where the pubic hair begins. It lies above the clitoris and below the belly button, just above the pubic symphysis. The fatty padding in this area comes in handy during face-to-face intercourse.

Labia Majora (Outer lips)   Coming down from the mons are the labia. The thick outer labia are called labia majora, and they are the part of a woman's genitals that are visible without her spreading her legs wide open. The labia majora often have hair on them, and their skin can be smooth or a bit ridged.

Labia Minora (Inner lips)   Open the outer labia and you will see the labia minora, which are typically not covered with hair. Some compare the appearance of the inner labia to flower petals. Like other parts of the vulva, the size, length, and color of the inner labia can vary greatly from woman to woman. They may be long and thick, or they may be barely visible, and they can vary in shade from pink to deep brown. It's also very common for the left and right labia to differ from each other in size and shape. All of these variations are completely normal. The labia minora are rich in nerve endings that contribute to sexual pleasure, and they also help to protect the vaginal opening when a woman's legs are together.

Clitoris   The clitoris is the small protrusion just above the urethral opening (where urine comes out), where the labia minora come together. The clitoris is similar in structure to a man's penis, and it is usually a woman's most sensitive sexual organ. In some women, the clitoris is barely visible; in others, it can be over an inch long. The clitoris is usually covered by the clitoral hood; retraction of the clitoral hood will expose the clitoris, which may be too sensitive for direct touch. Although only a small part of the clitoris is visible from the surface, the clitoral body is several inches long and dives deep inside the body. Inside a woman, the clitoris divides into two legs or "crura," which reach the G-spot on the anterior (front) wall of the vagina. Clitoral sensitivity varies from woman to woman.

Vagina   The vagina is the hollow, interior sexual organ that receives the penis during sexual intercourse. The vaginal opening lies between the urethral opening and the anus, and between the two labia minora. In young women, the vagina may be covered with the hymen, a thin membrane that is either perforated during sex (or other vigorous activity) or may dissolve with time. The G-spot lies within the vagina on the anterior wall, about one to three inches in. The

G-spot can be difficult to find, but when stimulated, it can be a source of immense pleasure and can lead to deep, whole-body orgasms. Prolonged stimulation can lead to multiple orgasms and even to the ejaculation of a clear, odorless fluid from the urethra. The vagina ends at the cervix, which is the opening to the uterus.

Cervix   The part of the uterus that connects to the vagina is known as the cervix. Often called the neck or entrance to the womb, the cervix lets menstrual blood out of, and semen into, the uterus.

Perineum   The female perineum is the area between the labia majora and the anus. During arousal, the perineum can become sensitive and receptive to stimulation and pleasure.

PC Muscle   The vagina is surrounded by a sling of muscle called the pubococcygeus muscle (or "PC muscle" for short). This muscle plays a vital part in sexual pleasure, and control of it can help women learn to tighten around an object inserted into the vagina. Once a woman locates the PC muscle, she can do special exercises called Kegels (page 178) to strengthen and control it.

Anus   Although it isn't always thought of as a part of a woman's sexual anatomy, the anus can be a site of great sexual pleasure, and many women enjoy anal play as part of their sexual repertoire. If an object is inserted into the anus and the anterior (front) wall is stimulated, these sensations can be transmitted to the vagina and can cause sexual pleasure.

I suggest that both partners get together with a mirror and a flashlight and try to locate each of these landmarks on the woman (aside from the cervix and G-spot, which would take some dedicated searching to spot). If you don't know your anatomy, pleasuring a woman would be like trying to climb into the cockpit of a plane without knowing what all the buttons do—or even where they are. In order to be a good lover, you need a good understanding of the sexual landmarks.

And knowing this information is good for women, too, because the better they know where things are down there, the better they will be at guiding their partner to the right spots. Be aware that your sexual landmarks may look different from the ones in the illustrations. Don't worry. They're still there!

Slippery When Wet: A Note on Lubes

Sometimes the female's natural ability to self-lubricate isn't enough, especially when employing handiwork. And that's why lubes were invented. Use them! For whatever reason, some people dislike the thought of using artificial lubricants. To them I say, "Get over it!" Get a couple of bottles of pure silicone lube and keep them in your bedside drawer. Once you use them, you'll be converting others. See the supplemental section on lubes (page 198) for more information.

As far as the details on how to pleasure a woman, I could provide chapter after chapter of details on each and every technique. In fact, that will be the topic of another book. But I will go ahead and give you a few generalizations.

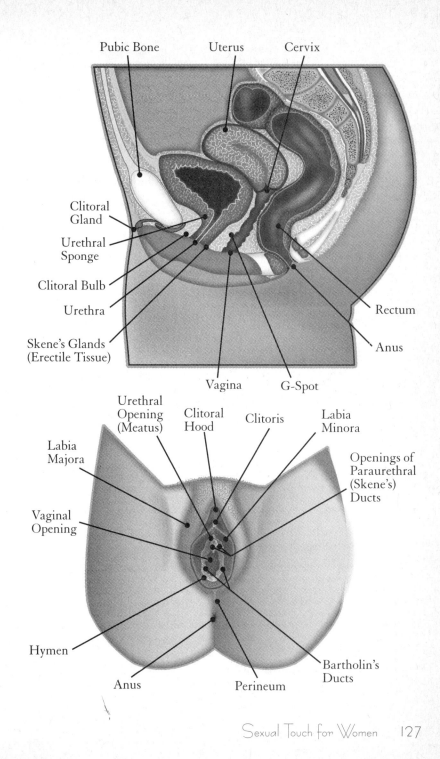

Pubic Bone   Uterus   Cervix

Clitoral Gland
Urethral Sponge
Clitoral Bulb
Urethra
Skene's Glands (Erectile Tissue)

Rectum
Anus

Vagina   G-Spot

Urethral Opening (Meatus)   Clitoral Hood   Clitoris   Labia Minora

Labia Majora

Openings of Paraurethral (Skene's) Ducts

Vaginal Opening

Hymen

Anus   Perineum

Bartholin's Ducts

To Pleasure a Woman

When you are pleasuring a woman, there are a few principles that you should know. These aren't hard-and-fast rules, but you need to know them before you can know when to break them. Unless you discover otherwise, the stimulation should go from broad to narrow, slow to fast, and light to deep.

BROAD TO NARROW

Begin with arousing her whole body. In this regard, men and women are different. Many men have a hard time enjoying full-body contact and massage right away, and want their partner to go straight for their penis. With a woman, you usually should warm up the whole body and arouse her before she's interested in genital touch. Think back to what you learned in the previous exercises in this book.

Once you've actually begun genital touch, start with a broad focus and then slowly narrow in. It's usually much better to open with a stroke that stimulates the whole vulva than to instantly zero in on the clitoris. So you might start with strokes that go all the way from the mons pubis to the perineum, then gradually narrow your scope to the outer lips, then to the inner lips, and finally from there to being more focused on the clitoris.

SLOW TO FAST

You also don't want to start out with fast, choppy, or jittery strokes. There may come a time for quick, lapping flicks and strokes, but the beginning of a session is not the time for that.

Before a woman is fully aroused, quick strokes may just irritate her and impair further arousal.

LIGHT TO DEEP

The amount of pressure you put into your strokes will also vary throughout your lovemaking. Pushing too hard right away can lead to pain and overstimulation, so start soft. As she becomes more aroused, she will be more accepting of a firmer touch.

SURPRISE HER

And remember, with each of these guidelines, it's not a linear progression. While you should follow the general trend of broad to narrow, slow to fast, and light to deep, you need to let the tides rise and fall. If when you speed up, you're not getting the response you expect, slow it back down for a while. Experiment and keep it fun!

Female Pleasure Techniques

Because women differ so greatly in their sexual tastes, I can't give you the exact formula for success. Determining which techniques she likes will have to be something that you figure out together. Communication is critical here. Let her show and teach you. Be eager for correction. If you get defensive, she will shut down, either because her feelings are hurt or because she's afraid of hurting yours. Neither of you can expect to become masters at this without teaching each other.

The best way to learn what she likes is to have her show you with her own hands. Or if she's willing to take a little longer, she can give you feedback as you do a little trial and error with your hands on her. Or why not try a combination of the two as you lay your hands on top of hers or vice versa? And as always, use a lot of lube.

Just as with the men, there are countless names for an infinite variety of techniques such as the wave, the squeeze, the slide, the smear, the figure eight, the pinch, the swirl, and more. As you learn what works for her, feel free to make up your own names, but know that combinations of various techniques may be what works best.

Exercise: Manual Pleasure for Her

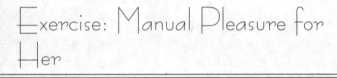

- ⚘ Find time when you and your wife can be alone for a while.
- ⚘ Wash your hands well and make sure that your nails are well-clipped and filed. Make sure that there are no sharp or rough spots.
- ⚘ Both of you undress. Begin performing the Arousing Touch exercise (page 107), so that you are beginning to more purposefully arouse your partner.
- ⚘ Lubricate your hands well and begin stroking her vulva. Remember, go from broad to narrow, soft to deep, and slow to fast. Also, remember to mix things up.

§ Practice making variations in tempo, pressure, and position. Make note of what your wife seems to like best so that you can discuss it later. Also, try your different techniques at different levels of arousal. Your wife may love one stroke at the beginning, but not later. There may be some strokes that she likes at the end, but not the beginning. And there may even be techniques that feel good in the middle, but not at either the beginning or the end.

§ Be present, and really focus on the sensations of your partner's genitals under your hands. Being in the moment is a way of showing respect, and it will enhance the experience for both you and your partner.

§ Stroke your wife for as long as you both would like. Don't make orgasm be the goal.

§ When you finish, hold each other and talk about the experience. Make notes of techniques you would like to try again.

Chapter 11

The Joys of Non-Orgasmic Intercourse

The title of this chapter may sound like a bit of a letdown to some guys, but be patient with me. We're going to start by talking about sex positions and give you some fun exercises to do with them, then we'll get into what I mean by "non-orgasmic intercourse" and why I'm teaching it here. I hope it's obvious that when I say "intercourse," I mean penile-vaginal sex. I'm also going to assume that you know that it's common for one or both partners to thrust and gyrate during intercourse. I actually had one couple come to me who did not know that, so if you didn't think that thrusting and gyrating were necessary during intercourse, you're not alone.

Sex Positions

This would be the point in the book where I'd propose a number of sex positions. I'd like to emphasize that while the ability to have sex in different positions is fun and can definitely add some zing to your sex life, you don't need to be a gymnast. It's not some competition where if you can master all of the positions then you "win at sex." Each of the positions is good for different things and at different times, and some work especially well for a given couple's specific fit.

So, while I encourage you to experiment and to shake things up, I also want you to realize that if you find that there are one or two positions that you especially like and use the majority of the time, you're not weird. It's very common for a couple to have a few positions that are their favorites. But if you're willing to explore other options, you may find something you both like better or are willing to allow for one another. Even when a new position or experience fails for both of you, it can be fun to get a good laugh as you realize that *Cosmo* magazine doesn't know what it's talking about.

I'm not going to mention all possible positions—there are other books for that—but I will comment on a few of the more obvious ones and why you may want to consider them as you do the exercise on page 136 of this chapter.

MAN ON TOP

The most common sexual position in Western society is what has been called the "missionary position." In this position, the woman lies on her back and the man lies on top of her between her legs. He holds himself up with his arms and guides his penis into her vagina.

This position allows for intimacy because you're face-to-face. But it's not great at providing G-spot stimulation because the man's arms are used for holding himself up and the penis is angled away from the G-spot. However, if a man inserts his penis and then moves *up* on the woman (toward her head), when he thrusts, he may be able to provide clitoral stimulation with the shaft of his penis or with his pubic bone. This is known as the Coital Alignment Technique.

While the basic missionary position is fairly simple, there are a lot of ways that couples can vary it and change the sensation. If a woman moves her legs closer together or farther apart, it will affect the tightness of her vagina and the depth of penetration. A woman can also experiment with how her legs are positioned vertically. Placing her legs flat against the bed will provide a different experience than bending her knees. The woman can also place her legs around her partner's hips or back and use them to pull him in as he thrusts. If she is very flexible, she can place her knees over her partner's shoulders.

There are also things that men can do to change the position. The height at which a man holds himself, and whether he uses his elbows or hands to prop himself up will change things. Similarly, the experience will be different depending on how much the man arches his back. If he rises up slightly on his knees, he can use them to push his partner's legs farther apart, which will intensify the sensation for both.

In the majority of man-on-top positions, the woman's hands are completely free. She should use this to her advantage.

WOMAN ON TOP

Another common variety of sexual position has the woman on top, and is often referred to as the "cowgirl." In the basic position, the man lies on his back. Facing his head, the woman kneels or squats over him to receive his penis. In woman-on-top positions, the woman is in control of the thrusting, and she can go as deep or as shallow as she wants. This position also gives the man great visuals.

This position requires a certain amount of leg strength and endurance for the woman, whereas the man is in more of the passive role. From this position, the woman can lean forward and rest on her arms to aid in her thrusting, or she can lean backward in order to have more penis stimulation of her G-spot.

In woman-on-top positions, the man's hands are free, and he should use them, whether it's for providing additional stimulation or to help steady and guide her. Women should be cautious with how they move while on top, because his penis is in a somewhat vulnerable position. Be careful that you don't damage it as you move around.

REAR ENTRY

This position doesn't allow a couple to see each other's faces, and some women may find this position emotionally or psychologically demeaning even if it is one of the more physically rewarding positions for them—when a woman is facedown with her buttocks elevated and the man enters her from behind, the head of his penis can very directly impact her G-spot, which can be very sexually satisfying for her.

Because he can't easily read her body language, and because he must do most of the thrusting, she must be very willing to communicate her desires and status so that she is appropriately satisfied.

There are numerous other positions, such as side-by-side, butterfly, standing variations, etc., and there's no dearth of books to provide you with suggestions and guides. One of the safer ones that I recommend is *Position of the Day* by Nerve.com.

Exercise: Playing with Positions

Sometimes experimenting with new positions or techniques can bring with it a little performance anxiety. (Or my mentioning performance anxiety can bring performance anxiety.) If this occurs, just turn this session into an Arousing Touch (page 107) or Sensual Touch (page 96) session, with positions.

§ Get naked and do some abbreviated warm-up activities (aka "foreplay") from earlier chapters. As you get into position, let each other know if you notice some potential obstacles and make adjustments along the way. (And as always, don't forget the lube!)

§ It's okay to feel awkward or laugh, and it's natural to bumble through this part. Just enjoy being together.

ß When you're ready, try for penetration. If you make it, wonderful! Thrust and enjoy stimulation for as long as you would like. Watch each other for cues and talk through it as much as you'd both like. Achieving orgasm in a new position can be difficult at first. The sensations are unfamiliar, and different muscles are being used, so don't let orgasm be your goal. Your goal is to feel and enjoy. This makes failure almost impossible.

Thrusting for Him

I'm not going to assume anything here. When you get into position and get your penis in her vagina, now what? Just thrusting over and over at the same intensity and speed can be dull or even irritating to a woman. You have to vary things up. (This is in addition to saying loving words, having appropriate eye contact, using your hands, requesting feedback, etc.)

When you start thrusting, unless you know she wants otherwise, start slow. If she's not super turned on and ready, moving fast could be more painful than pleasurable. One thing you can try is very small, slow thrusts, each time going slightly farther than the time before. This can gradually open up her vagina. This will also give a fun, teasing aspect to penetration, leaving her wanting more.

As things get heated up, try varying the patterns of your strokes and speeds; be inventive. Men tend to thrust in the way that feels good to them, not necessarily in the way they think the woman wants. Quite frankly, you'll probably enjoy almost anything that happens while your penis is inside her vagina, so you might as well do what makes *her* feel good, right? When *she* has a good time, *you'll* have a good time.

Try mixing tempos and the depth of thrusting. Long, smooth thrusts can feel very good for her and be extremely arousing. Alternatively, there are a lot of nerve endings just in the first couple inches of the vagina, so you can get a lot of mileage out of short thrusts. Ideally, you're going to mix the action between short thrusts and long thrusts. You may try something like a few shallow, then one deep. If you really want to try something interesting, try this Taoist prescription: begin with nine short strokes and one deep. Then perform eight short strokes and two deep. Then seven short and three deep. Continue in this fashion until you are doing ten deep strokes.

Furthermore, know that there's more that you can do than simply thrusting in and out. When women are in control during sex (as in woman on top), they often roll their hips and move from side to side in a grinding fashion. There's a reason for this—they like how it feels. Rolling their hips allows them to feel the sensation of your penis in a variety of different places in their vagina. You can do the same. Try circling your hips while you're inside your woman and notice how she responds.

Experiment with the angle of thrust as well. Consider altering the direction of your thrust so you're aiming more toward the anterior (tummy) side of the vagina, which will provide more direct G-spot stimulation.

So, experiment and try new things, but keep it fun. Don't get so caught up thinking about your thrusting that you end up making it a rote routine. Do what feels natural and good, and stay in the moment.

Thrusting for Her

Ladies, my advice to you is simple: "Do what feels good to you." There is very little that you can do that he will dislike, so just focus on the motions that give you pleasure. Obviously, you'll be more in control if you're on top. But there's also a lot that you can do when you're underneath him—you don't have to remain still and be passive. Try rolling or tilting your hips or moving your legs to different positions. When you do this, his penis will engage you in slightly different ways. You can also engage in a little bit of gentle "domination." Even though he's in the position of physical control, you can be the one to provide verbal instructions to him as to what you would like him to do to you.

When you're in physical control, listen to your body and move according to what feels good. Moving allows you to control your own sexual experience and forces you to stay in the moment and focus on your sensations. As an added bonus, your moving will be a definite turn-on for him. Men love seeing signs of arousal in women, and feeling you wriggling, bucking, rolling, or thrusting will definitely be arousing. But remember, you're not doing this just as a show for him. You're doing this for your enjoyment. Focusing on your pleasure will feel better for you, and because your arousal will be authentic, it will also be the most erotic for him.

Because some women are not yet sufficiently connected to their sexual selves, they have a hard time actually knowing what feels good. The following exercise will help you to learn more about the motions and sensations that you find pleasurable during intercourse.

Exercise: Non-Orgasmic Intercourse

Just as the Sensual Touch exercise (page 96) was about pleasure without arousal, this lesson is on sex without orgasm. For men, this may seem not only foreign, but appalling! You may insist that the purpose of sex is to have an orgasm, but as long as it's still fun and pleasurable, it doesn't have to always be about the orgasm. For some men and women, the expectation and pressure of having an orgasm can cause anxiety and overshadow what should be a shared intimate experience, regardless of outcome.

- Using the techniques described in the previous chapters, arouse each other until he has an erection. (If he does not obtain an erection, return to the previous exercises or use the alternatives mentioned in this exercise.)
- While he lies on his back, mount him and insert his penis into your vagina.
- Allow the erect penis to rest in your vagina while you contract and relax your PC muscle against it. (For more information on this

muscle, see "Orgasmic Mastery for Women" on page 165.) Note how the sensation changes as you tense and relax.

⅛ Slowly begin to move up and down on your partner's penis. Play and experiment with different motions and movements.

⅛ Do what feels good for you, and only be motivated by your own feelings. Don't chase his pleasure. You need to temporarily be "selfish" so you can learn to feel and enjoy your vaginal sensations. Don't worry. He'll love it, too, I promise.

⅛ If your partner becomes too excited, he should tell you, and you should take a short break to avoid ejaculation. You can either just hold still with his penis inside your vagina, or you can withdraw and then reinsert when he has regained control.

⅛ During the rest periods, you or your partner may want to stimulate your clitoris so that you do not lose arousal.

⅛ It is normal for a man to lose his erection during this exercise either due to prolonged stimulation or ejaculation.

⅛ The exercise is complete when you feel satisfied that you have learned more about your vaginal sensations and when he learns to enjoy the act of intercourse without requiring ejaculation. This teaches both of you control.

Blue Balls

It's a crass term and not technically correct—I didn't coin it. "Blue balls" is a dull, aching sensation that can occur in a man's testicles when he gets aroused but doesn't ejaculate. It can actually be quite painful and last for hours or more. A man may experience it when he unintentionally becomes aroused or when the arousal is prolonged without subsequent ejaculation. Women can experience something similar when their G-spot is intensely stimulated for a prolonged period.

Gentlemen, you may be concerned about causing this uncomfortable sensation when engaging in non-orgasmic sex. Unfortunately, there isn't really a way to avoid or prevent this from happening. But once sexual activity is stopped, the pain will gradually pass—it won't kill you. The ache can also be treated by ejaculating, but that is not the goal here. Unless the pain is severe, my suggestion is to just wait it out. I don't recommend using masturbation as a form of relief, as this can interfere with the benefits of the exercise. In cases of severe pain, the couple can discuss resolving it by allowing the man to orgasm, but this should only be used in cases of extreme discomfort.

The purpose of non-orgasmic sex is to enjoy intercourse for the sake of intercourse and not for the sake of orgasm. The benefits of this exercise should outweigh any discomfort you may feel from "blue balls," and you shouldn't use this discomfort as an excuse for always "needing release." Do your best, boys, and I promise that the long-term benefits will outweigh the temporary discomfort.

Chapter 12

Orgasmic Mastery for Men

Erection, then ejaculation and orgasm. Most men think there's no alternative pathway. For most men, this is the easiest route, but it's not the only one. Erection and ejaculation occur in the penis. An orgasm occurs in the mind. Women know this—and we'll chat about the female versions in a later chapter. But for a guy, it sure does make orgasm easier if you can follow the traditional path.

Assuming that you can achieve regular erections, there are some mastery techniques that you can pursue. Later, I'll explain what you're going to do with these skills. If you can't wait to know, you're welcome to skip ahead and see what treats I have in store for you, but be sure to come back here and learn how to do this. Knowing *about* something and actually *doing* it are two very different things.

Kegels

There are some specific exercises that can help men to improve the quality of their erections and assist with ejaculatory control. The first is the humble Kegel exercise. Many men think of Kegels as women's exercises (if they know what a Kegel is at all). However, Kegel exercises can be just as beneficial for men, as they help men to achieve more intense orgasms, increased ejaculation power, stronger erections, decreased risk of incontinence, and better sexual control. They can even help men learn to experience multiple male orgasms. (We'll cover that later in this chapter, on page 157.)

Kegeling involves tensing the muscles of the pelvic floor (including the pubococcygeus or "PC" muscle). You can find this muscle by stopping the stream when you're urinating. Practice clenching the PC muscle to stop the flow the next several times you're using the restroom. This will help you identify this muscle. Practice isolating this muscle, so that you're not tensing your buttocks or abdomen at all, just your pelvic floor.

Once you've figured this out, you can practice Kegels everywhere: at the grocery store, in the car, or during a boring business meeting. Since you never break a sweat, the possibilities are limitless.

Exercise: Kegel

Kegel Variation 1

- ⑤ Contract the PC muscle.
- ⑤ Hold while you count to ten.
- ⑤ Relax the PC muscle.
- ⑤ Repeat for as many repetitions as you can. Try to do at least ten reps.
- ⑤ Repeat several times each day, every day.

Kegel Variation 2

- ⑤ Gradually contract the PC muscle from relaxed to as tight as possible for a count of five.
- ⑤ Relax the PC muscle for one count.
- ⑤ Repeat.

Kegel Variation 3

- ⑤ Gradually contract the PC muscle from relaxed to as tight as possible for a count of five, then relax for one count.
- ⑤ Contract the PC muscle fast and tight for one count. Relax for one count, and repeat.
- ⑤ Contract the PC muscle fast and tight for one count. Relax for a count of ten.
- ⑤ Tighten the PC slightly for a count of five, then tighten it more for another count of five. Tighten the PC completely for a count of five.

§ Relax the PC only slightly for a count of five, then relax it a little more for another count of five. Completely relax the muscle for a count of five.

As with any form of exercise, you should make sure you are performing Kegels properly and isolating the correct muscles. This will give you the quickest and best results. Remember, while performing Kegel exercises, you should not be flexing your upper leg muscles, buttocks, or abdominal muscles. The only muscle you want to be contracting is your PC muscle. If you feel your anus tensing while exercising, don't worry. It may be difficult at first to tighten the PC muscle and anus separately. Eventually, you should be able to contract the PC muscle by itself.

If you get headaches while exercising, this may be a sign that you are tensing your chest muscles or holding your breath. Make sure to breathe deeply and slowly. If you find the exercises tiring or if you experience back or stomach pain after you exercise, then you are probably, a) trying too hard, and b) using your stomach muscles. If you do feel any pain, make an appointment with your sexologist or physician to look into the matter. Pain usually implies that the techniques aren't being performed properly; a qualified doctor should be able to correct you, or at the very least find out if there is anything wrong.

Exercise: Pelvic Floor Relaxation

Like Kegels, pelvic floor relaxation is something you do by yourself. In the Kegel exercises, you practiced tensing your pelvic floor. This is an important skill, and a strong pelvic floor can give you great dividends sexually. However, it's just as important to be able to relax your pelvis. The pelvic floor muscles surround the base of the penis, and if you're constantly tensing them, you may be interfering with the blood flow to your penis, which would impede erections.

Your body tightens in response to the pressures, tensions, and burdens of life, and this often includes unconsciously tensing your pelvic muscles. By learning to relax your pelvic floor, you give your body the foundation for easier erections. And if your pelvic muscles relax, the rest of your body will follow.

- Assume a comfortable position and relax.
- Contract your pelvic muscles and hold for three seconds.
- Then relax and stay relaxed for five to ten seconds.
- Then relax further. This second relaxation is done five to ten seconds after the first relaxation because it takes that long for the basal tone of the muscles to give way. It's like coming down the stairs to the ground floor and then realizing that you can descend into the basement.

- Once you've allowed your pelvis to fully relax, notice how you can feel the blood flowing to the area, but don't allow yourself to tense as you focus your mind on your pelvis.
- Throughout this exercise, consciously focus on the sensations. Feel what it feels like to be tense, and feel what it feels like to relax.
- Repeat five times.

Exercise: Wax and Wane

I suggest that you do this exercise together. This exercise is performed in several steps. You may find it necessary to perform some of the first steps a couple of times on yourself before you master the skills enough to direct your spouse on how to help. Be patient and give yourself all the time you need.

It's not mandatory, but you might consider performing the Sensual Touch exercise on page 96 before proceeding with this exercise.

Step 1: Soothing Genital Touch

- Rest on your back and ask your partner to gently and soothingly explore your testicles and penis with soft, slow touch for a few minutes.
- Relax your pelvic muscles and focus on your feelings.

- Your wife can give you soft, featherlike caresses to pleasure your penis without producing an erection.
- Relax and concentrate on the calm sensations.

Step 2: Finding Your Calm, Easy Erection

- In this step of the exercise, you will practice getting an erection with self-entrancement arousal—maximum body relaxation, minimal touch, and a focus on your sensations (not on fantasy or interactions with your partner).
- After performing Step 1 for a few minutes, ask her to very gradually increase her stimulation. You are trying to find the minimum amount of stimulation you need to get an erection. If she needs guidance, help her.
- Do not force an erection. Assuming that you don't have erectile dysfunction, your body knows how to get an erection all on its own, as long as you get your mind out of the way. Just let the erection happen by keeping your pelvic muscles relaxed and focusing on the pleasures you're feeling. The more relaxed and focused you are, the more easily you will become erect.
- It's okay if it takes a long time for an erection to begin. Do not force it or you will become distracted and undermine your relaxation.
- While you lie still and focus on your feelings, you or your partner should continue to gradu-

ally increase the stimulation. Take it slow and let your body respond. If you're in too much of a rush, not only are you not focusing on your sensations, but you could give more stimulation than is really necessary.

§ Once you start to get an erection, reduce the stimulation. Let your erection completely subside, then slowly increase stimulation again.

§ Repeat this step until you feel confident in your ability to calmly, easily get an erection without overthinking it or working at it.

Step 3: Choosing to Wax and Wane

§ After performing Step 2 and gaining and losing an erection several times, have your partner gently stimulate you to erection.

§ With your partner continuing to stimulate you, maintain that erection for at least three minutes. Remember, this requires no work on your part. Your partner will do the stimulating, and your body provides the erection. All you do is let it happen.

§ After at least three minutes, let your erection subside by about 50 percent by having her back down on the stimulation.

§ As you feel your erection subsiding, stay focused on your sensations.

§ When your erection has gone down by about 50 percent, signal to her to change the touch to gradually bring back a relaxed erection.

- ♪ Notice that when you're physically relaxed, it is easier to regain your erection. Even if you lose your erection, you can regain it easily when you are calm and focused.
- ♪ Repeat this exercise until you feel confident in your ability to get, maintain, and regain an erection.

Premature Ejaculation

Watch TV sitcoms and you'll find premature ejaculation jokes aplenty. But like most supposedly hilarious jokes, some guys experience real mental anguish over it. Although the term gets thrown around a lot, there's no absolute definition of how fast is too fast, as it ends up being pretty subjective.

In the end, premature ejaculation just means ejaculating earlier than you and your partner would've wanted for your mutual satisfaction. So what might be considered premature by one couple might be perfect timing for another. And what might be premature in one situation for a couple may become irrelevant if they learn additional techniques to satisfy them both.

To a certain extent, much of what is considered "premature ejaculation" exists mostly in men's minds. They may think that "real men" can pump away for hours and hours without ejaculating. This may be a fantasy of yours, but when it comes to the real world, most women and men don't want to plateau for that long. According to surveys, the average amount of time spent in intercourse is three to ten minutes. So for some couples, "curing premature ejaculation" is as simple as resetting their expectations regarding how long intercourse should last.

However, for some men, there really is a significant gap between how long he *wants* intercourse to last and how long he *can* last. These men should first take a deep breath and calm down. There's no reason why they should get worked up over this. Every man has, on occasion, ejaculated sooner than he or his partner wished. If you ejaculate too soon for your partner to experience orgasm during intercourse, know that almost all women require additional stimulation besides intercourse to climax.

According to Dr. Ian Kerner, author of *She Comes First*, only 20 percent of women can orgasm from intercourse alone. You'll need to give her additional stimulation to get her to climax anyway. My advice is to provide that stimulation to her prior to intercourse so that you can strive to both orgasm at about the same time, but if you still orgasm before she does, be a gentleman and keep providing stimulation to her—don't just roll over and go to sleep.

Some men who struggle with premature ejaculation find that increasing their frequency of ejaculation improves their staying power. In addition to making you feel irritable and tense, going for long periods of time without sex can increase your likelihood of ejaculating after just a thrust or two. If you start having more regular sex, your body may relax and trust that it doesn't need to ejaculate quite as quickly.

To address premature ejaculation, one of the best things I can advise, but hardest for you to follow, is for you to get rid of performance anxiety. Performance anxiety is detrimental in a couple of ways. First, it increases stress, which hastens the ejaculatory response. Second, it takes you out of your body and into your mind, which can make you miss the subtle (and not-so-subtle) cues that your body gives you as it's getting close to orgasm.

If you slow down and focus on sensations, you'll know when you're getting close, and you can vary your stroke accordingly. This is why it's such a cruel irony that men often try to delay their orgasm by thinking about unsexy things like baseball or their grandmother. Not only does this make sex less fun (and possibly gets you feeling strangely aroused when it's the ninth inning and the bases are loaded), it usually doesn't work!

The following exercise will help you to gain confidence in your ability to last longer. It will teach you to tune in to your sensations and to watch for the signs that ejaculation is imminent.

Exercise: Male Ejaculation Control

This exercise is most easily performed by the man stimulating himself because it relies on him tuning in and quickly interpreting his own sensations. However, it can also be performed as a couple. I know that some of my readers have strong feelings regarding self-stimulation, and if you have strongly held objections, I don't want to push you to do something distressful. (I assume that you've read the chapter on this topic [page 21] earlier in the book.)

However, I would like you to remember that the purpose of this exercise is to help a man overcome premature ejaculation in order to experience greater intimacy with his spouse. In this regard, you may prefer to use terms like "self-cultivation" or "self-exploration" to the more socially charged term of "masturbation."

Even if you're fine with self-stimulation, I would encourage you to involve your spouse wherever possible. After all, sex is about connecting and experiencing love as a couple, and this type of experience can feel very intimate and bring a couple closer to each other.

This exercise can also work with only the woman doing the touching, but it may take more time because not only does it involve the learning curves of two different people, it also requires accurate communication and appropriate responses.

The instructions assume that the man is doing this solo. If you're doing this together, simply make appropriate changes as you follow the directions. Whichever way you perform this exercise, it will help you to experience greater control over ejaculation.

When you perform this exercise, take a little time to relax and let go of tension and unnecessary thoughts. I suggest performing a Sensual Touch (page 96) or Relaxation (page 85) exercise first.

Step 1: Identifying the Point of No Return

⚶ When you feel calm and relaxed, stimulate yourself or have her stimulate you until you have a full erection.

⚶ During both parts of this exercise, use fantasy only as much as is absolutely necessary. Let the erection occur from stimulation rather than your imagination. Once you're erect, focus on physical sensations and not on fantasy.

⚶ Stroke the penis in a way that approximates vaginal penetration. As your arousal grows, pay attention to the physical sensations in your penis and pelvic area.

⚶ Notice the sensations that happen just prior to ejaculation. Discover where your point of no return is, the point after which ejaculation is inevitable. There should be some sensations of tingling or tightness that occur while it is still possible to stop ejaculation.

⚶ Don't stop yourself from ejaculating. Just recognize the sensations and feelings in your body that immediately precede ejaculation. Do this for at least the next three times that you have an orgasm. Once you can tell when the tingling sensations arrive just before the point of no return, you're ready to continue the exercise.

Step 2: At the Edge

- ♂ Stroke the penis until erect and continue until the pre-ejaculatory tingling arrives, then stop the stimulation for at least 15 seconds and concentrate on letting the feelings of arousal decrease.

- ♂ When arousal has receded and ejaculation is no longer imminent, begin to stroke the penis again. When you feel yourself getting close to ejaculation, stop until you feel you are back in control. When you stop stimulation, you may find that your penis begins to soften and lose its erection. This is common and nothing to be worried about.

- ♂ You may also find that performing a Kegel squeeze at the time of tingling can put the brakes on ejaculation. But for some men, performing a Kegel actually intensifies sensation and pushes them closer to the edge. Experiment to see what a properly timed Kegel does for you.

- ♂ When arousal has sunk in again, start stimulating the penis once more. When back at the brink of ejaculation, back down again. Do this for a total of three times.

- ♂ After you have done this three times, permit yourself to orgasm and ejaculate.

- ♂ If, during this exercise, you misjudge and accidentally start to ejaculate, don't stress out and don't try to stop it. Just enjoy the experiment, and use what you learned to be in better control next time.

꿍 Each time you repeat this exercise, increase the number of times that you can perform the start/stop cycle before ejaculating. Try to get to six cycles.

꿍 By doing these cycles, you will learn how to tolerate stimulation for longer periods of time before needing to stop, as well as how to regain control faster during stops.

꿍 Practice this exercise in different positions (such as the ones in which you frequently have sex). Doing this will teach you different lessons about ejaculation control.

꿍 When you feel confident performing this technique with hands, try this exercise during intercourse. Be aware that your partner's vagina will probably be much more arousing than your hands, and don't be discouraged if at first you have setbacks. In time, you will learn to control your arousal, even inside your partner.

Male Multiple Orgasms

All right, this is the part you were excited about, right? (If you skipped ahead to this section, you'll need to master the previous exercises before mastering male multiple orgasms.) When it comes to multiple orgasms, men and women are a little different. Most women have the natural ability to have multiple orgasms (lucky us!). This is partly because we women don't need to ejaculate to experience an orgasm. Because women don't naturally ejaculate, and because an orgasm is in the mind, the mind does not need a rest period before it can climax again.

In contrast, male ejaculation does require that the genital system have a brief pause (called the refractory period) before the penis can become erect and ejaculate again. The length of the refractory period varies from man to man—anywhere from a few minutes to hours—and it tends to lengthen with age.

However, if a man can learn, as women innately know, to separate ejaculation from orgasm, and focus on pleasure rather than expulsion, he can develop the ability to have multiple orgasms in a row.

LAYING THE GROUNDWORK

Before we get into exactly how you can experience multiple orgasms, we have to lay a little bit of groundwork and talk about what multiple orgasms are and how the multi-orgasmic response cycle differs from the typical male sexual response cycle. The typical response cycle consists of an excitement phase, then a plateau phase, followed by peaking at orgasm and ejaculation, and then moves quickly down into resolution. A refractory period follows before the cycle can be repeated.

Specific physiological signals accompany each stage in the male sexual cycle. In the excitement stage, the penis becomes partially erect, and the testicles swell and are usually pulled upward toward the perineum as the scrotal skin tenses and thickens. Muscle tension increases, as do heart rate and breathing. The face and chest may become flushed, and the nipples may become erect. The first drops of clear pre-ejaculate fluid may begin to secrete from the penis. The excitement stage lasts for at least a minute or two, or it can last for several hours.

Plateau is the next phase, in which the body prepares for orgasm. Like excitement, this phase lasts for varying lengths of time. During this period, all of the physiologic changes from the previous stage become more pronounced. Heart rate, breathing, and muscle tension all intensify. The testicles pull up even closer to the body, and the penis and testicles may increase in size again. Secretion of pre-ejaculate may intensify. Muscle spasms may begin to occur throughout the body.

When the sexual excitement elevates beyond plateau, he enters orgasm. This phase is characterized by intense physical pleasure and the rhythmic contraction of the pelvic muscles. In the typical male response cycle, orgasm is immediately followed by ejaculation. As orgasm begins, semen first pools at the base of the penis, then is ejected outward.

After a man has ejaculated, he enters the resolution phase, which is characterized by feelings of satisfaction and satiety. The urgency brought on by arousal disappears, as do most of the physical signs of arousal. Heart rate and breathing reduce, and muscle tension disappears. Flushed skin returns to its normal color. The testicles drop down in the scrotum again, and the penis returns to its usual flaccid size. In the typical male, these changes take place quite rapidly.

The male multi-orgasmic cycle begins in the same way, moving from excitement through plateau to a point near ejaculation (the "point of no return" discussed in the last exercise), and it includes all of the same physiological signs of arousal. However, in the multi-orgasmic cycle, when the man spikes beyond plateau, he experiences a non-ejaculatory orgasm in the form of a series of genital contractions that typically last for about three to five seconds. (This is the typical orgasmic response for a woman.) These contractions may feel like a fluttering or wave of pleasure. Then, instead of dropping down into resolution, the multi-orgasmic cycle simply dips back down into the plateau stage, from which it can easily swing back up to orgasm again and again.

The orgasms that follow usually increase in strength as they go on. After experiencing several non-ejaculatory orgasms, a man may decide that he wants to ejaculate after his final orgasm. Even after gaining the ability to experience multiple non-ejaculatory orgasms, some men still desire the psychological pleasure of ejaculation. If a man decides to ejaculate with the final orgasm, then immediately after ejaculation he will drop into resolution and trigger the refractory period. As in the typical male sexual response cycle, the man will temporarily be unable to achieve another erection or receive further stimulation due to increased sensitivity to touch.

If the man decides not to ejaculate at all, his arousal pattern departs from the usual male cycle and actually much more closely resembles the typical female sexual response cycle. His arousal will then decline gradually over the course of about an hour, as opposed to dropping off sharply. There is no refractory period in this model, and a man can resume sexual play at any point he desires.

There are two big keys to gaining the ability to experience male multiple orgasms. The first is to *understand* that orgasm and ejaculation are distinct events, which, with effort, a man can learn to distinguish and separate. Orgasm is a euphoric experience of the mind associated with diffuse tingling and muscular fasciculation. Ejaculation is the process by which semen is expelled from the body. Most men assume that orgasm and ejaculation are one and the same because they happen in such rapid succession, with orgasm beginning slightly before ejaculation, then tapering off during ejaculation.

The second key to multiple orgasms involves gaining the *ability* to separate orgasm and ejaculation. The ability to separate these events involves precise use and timing of the PC muscle contractions—the same muscle used in Kegel exercises.

PREPARING YOURSELF

Having multiple orgasms as a man takes a great deal of desire, patience, and preparation. It requires an intimate knowledge of your own sexual response cycle (which can be gained through the Wax and Wane exercise described earlier in this chapter, on page 148) and a strong PC muscle (which can be developed through the Kegel exercises described earlier in this chapter, on page 145).

It's essential to become intimately familiar with your PC muscle so that you can learn to precisely control it. Some of this control will come with experience, and some will come by strengthening it through regular exercise. Practice the exercises in this section repeatedly until your PC muscle is as strong as iron. Then you will be ready to have multiple orgasms.

Exercise: Practicing for Multiples

- During your next sexual experience, stop stimulation just before you reach the point of no return (the point where you would ejaculate).
- Without stimulating your penis, contract and hold your PC muscle (page 115) for a count of ten.
- Relax and take a few minutes' break to let your arousal subside.
- Resume stimulation, this time bringing yourself just a bit closer to the point of no return.
- Again, stop stimulation. Contract and hold your PC muscle for a count of ten.
- Resume stimulation again, paying very special attention to your own state of arousal. This time, as you reach the point of no return, keep going until you reach orgasm.
- Right as you orgasm, you will experience several contractions that signal the beginning of ejaculation.
- Just before these contractions begin (but still during the orgasm), stop all stimulation to the penis and squeeze your PC muscle tight. You'll probably feel yourself trying to ejaculate, but hold it back! If you are successful, squeezing your PC muscle will effectively shut off your ejaculation, erasing your refractory period. A small amount of semen may seep out, but not

with any of the force you would normally experience during an unrestrained orgasm.

§ If you were able to hold off ejaculating after your orgasm, begin stimulation again now. It should feel as though you are still aroused, and not like you just ejaculated. You should be able to continue for a short time until you have another orgasm.

§ If you were unable to keep from ejaculating the first time, either your PC muscle isn't strong enough yet or you squeezed it too early or too late. If you begin squeezing too late (after the ejaculatory contractions have already begun), it is nearly impossible to stop the process completely. With practice, you will learn the timing.

═══════════════════════════════════════

I've known some men who have successfully learned how to have multiple orgasms, but who still prefer the satisfaction of knowing that they are ejaculating. That's probably the biggest reason that you don't hear about this becoming mankind's greatest goal.

If you really want to learn how to have multiple orgasms, keep practicing, be patient, and enjoy the ride! Becoming multi-orgasmic is something that takes a lot of practice. Keep at it, but don't let seeking multiple orgasms rob you of the joy of sex. Stay in the moment and don't get too goal-oriented. You'll get it eventually—plus, you'll have a lot of fun along the way!

Overcoming Obstacles to Multiple Orgasms

One of the biggest obstacles to becoming multi-orgasmic is the failure to squeeze the PC muscle tightly enough to ward off ejaculation. You may feel some contractions, but do not stop squeezing at this point. A few ejaculatory contractions are likely, even if you are successful. If you are doing it right, the contractions will stop before you ejaculate. If you can't hold your ejaculation back with your PC muscle, you need to practice your Kegels more (page 145).

Another common problem is failing to determine exactly where the boundaries of orgasm and ejaculation begin and end. If you cannot determine the difference between orgasm and ejaculation, a key to becoming multi-orgasmic, you can only succeed by accident. If you have trouble telling where ejaculation and orgasm start and stop, return to Wax and Wane (page 148), and keep practicing.

You'll find that you'll have the most success if you take it slow. Slowing down the stimulation allows you to discover your personal boundaries between arousal, plateau, and orgasm more easily. With a firm grasp on these aspects of your arousal, you will know much more clearly when to squeeze your PC muscle and stop stimulation, and when to relax your PC muscle and resume stimulation to experience another orgasm.

Chapter 13

Orgasmic Mastery for Women

It is ironic that while many of the sexual problems for men stem from their inability to hold orgasm back, many of the sexual problems for women come from their difficulty bringing on an orgasm. Women can worry because they either cannot climax or because they feel that it takes too much time or effort to do so. If this is you, please understand that women require quite a bit more stimulation and attention to orgasm than do their husbands. Women on average require between 15 and 30 minutes of stimulation before they start to climax. However long it takes you is however long it takes.

Now, if you have not yet experienced an orgasm, don't feel like you're alone. Studies indicate that some 30 percent of women have never climaxed. Scientists use the term "anorgasmic" to refer to a woman who doesn't experience orgasm. I encourage women not to think of themselves as anorgasmic, but *pre*-orgasmic. Your body was built for sex, and it has the ability to orgasm; you just need to learn how to let yourself experience it. And you're in luck, because I'm about to set you on a path to do just that.

Why Orgasm?

Believe it or not, I actually receive this question sometimes. Some women who don't orgasm are happy with their sex lives just the way they are. They either don't have much interest in sex, or they're happy to simply allow sex to be a way of pleasing their husbands. They get enjoyment from giving, but have difficulty receiving. Why rock the boat or change the status quo? They say they're satisfied with things just the way they are.

While I can understand this sentiment, I think it's important to realize that it actually can be a form of selfishness. These women are pleasing their husbands while avoiding their own issues. Consider this: If a woman never learns how to orgasm, then she's always in the position of giver. She never has to open up her needs to her husband, meaning that she will never feel vulnerable or rejected sexually. But intimacy is a two-way street, and if you never learn to let your husband give to you, your relationship will not be as strong or as close as it could be if you allowed him to give you what you desire.

The sad thing is that being the "selfless wife" can hurt both partners. Men sometimes grow bored or feel that they're being selfish if the focus is always on their satisfaction. Consciously or not, they may come to realize that their wives are, in some way, hiding from them. They may actually feel hurt because they are never allowed to give back. Women, I'll tell you a secret: gentlemen love to give women orgasms. Men enjoy the feelings of receiving great sex, but there's nothing that makes a man feel more masculine, worthwhile, and successful than *giving* great sex.

Similarly, women who have sex solely for their partners often grow bored, and even as they choose to exclusively give to their husbands, they may begin to feel put upon or resentful. Ladies, see if this sounds familiar: It's the end of a long day. You've been working, taking care of the kids, and now you're looking forward to a little downtime, but your husband wants sex, and now it just feels like another item on your to-do list. You already do so much for him; why does he want sex so incessantly?

Maybe you tell him "not tonight" because you're too tired to do him another favor, or maybe you grudgingly give in. And then if anything goes wrong during sex, it feels like a personal affront, like your favor isn't good enough. Because when sex is a task, it loses all of its joy.

If sex is to be good, it should be good for both partners. While this doesn't mean that each and every sexual encounter has to give both partners an orgasm, it does mean that there should be some balance to the exchange. Sometimes you'll have sex to please him. Sometimes he'll have sex to please you. Hopefully a lot of the time you'll have sex to please each other.

If you think that orgasm isn't for you, I hope you'll reconsider. Whether you're avoiding orgasm because of fear of failure, fear of intimacy, fear of your body, fear of the lack of control, or fear of your desires, I say to you, "Let go and try." Every woman is sexual. Every woman has the ability to receive and enjoy pleasure. It's part of your divine birthright. Don't bury your feminine talent. Claim it!

The Female Sexual Response Cycle

Before we can have orgasms, we have to know what they are and how to get there. Orgasm occurs at the peak of arousal in the human sexual response cycle. So let's talk about the female sexual response cycle and what that means for your orgasms.

The female sexual response cycle begins with excitement. This is the stage when you are first starting to be aroused and interested in sex. New studies seem to indicate that men and women can differ here. Men follow the expected pattern of becoming mentally aroused by something. They are then cognizant of this arousal, and then they manifest the signs of physical arousal. Women may be different. Women can become subconsciously aroused by something, then manifest the physical signs, and then become consciously aware of their aroused feelings. This means that your body may be ready for sex before your mind is.

But just like for men, arousal can be initiated by physical or mental stimulation, and it can last for a short time or for several hours. During this phase, your muscle tension increases, your heart rate and breathing accelerate, and your skin may become flushed, especially around the breasts. Blood flow increases to your genitalia, making your clitoris and inner lips swell. Your vagina also swells and begins to lubricate. Increased blood flow to the breasts causes your nipples to become hard and erect and your breasts to swell.

The plateau phase follows. It can be relatively short, or it can draw out for a long time. Ideally, you'll control the duration. In this phase, all of the changes that began in excitement continue to increase in intensity. The vagina continues to swell, and the coloration of the genitals changes. Because of the increased blood flow, the vagina often assumes a deep purple color. You may begin to experience muscle spasms in the face and elsewhere. At this point the clitoris becomes extremely sensitive. In some women, it becomes so sensitive that direct touch actually feels painful. To avoid painful overstimulation, the clitoris may withdraw under the clitoral hood. You may find yourself moaning or otherwise vocalizing during this stage.

The next phase is orgasm. This is the shortest stage in the sexual response cycle. In this stage, strong, involuntary muscle contractions rock through the pelvic floor, vagina, and uterus. You may also experience muscular contractions elsewhere in the body. These contractions, combined with a sense of euphoria and intense pleasure, make up the experience of orgasm.

As the contractions of orgasm fade away, you move into the stage of resolution. During this stage, the physical and mental signs of arousal slowly subside as the body returns to homeostasis. Generally, during resolution, there's a sense of peace, tranquility, closeness, and a feeling that all is right in the world. Unlike men, who need a refractory period before they can experience arousal or orgasm again, women can start having fun again right away. During the refractory period, men can feel sedate and ready for sleep; for women, the post-orgasm period may continue to be a time of excit-ability and alertness. If you resume stimulation, you could experience orgasm after orgasm.

And unlike men, who tend to be more limited in their range of orgasms, women can experience a variety of types of orgasms. There seems to be no end to the ways that women can experience orgasm: clitoral, vaginal, G-spot, nipple, oral, squirting, and mental orgasms, just to name a few. However, it's probably easiest to start out with the good-old clitoral orgasm.

Obstacles to Orgasm

So now that we've talked about what orgasm is and why we should have it, what are some of the obstacles to orgasm? Early in this book, we talked about some of the things that can inhibit sexual desire (page 12). These same issues can also seriously interfere with a woman's ability to orgasm. For a woman, climaxing requires totally letting go, and persistent feelings of sexual guilt (page 31) or worry can make let-ting go awfully hard to do. Stress and the inability to shut off one's thoughts can also lead to difficulty achieving orgasm. For those who have difficulty tuning out the world, return to doing the Relaxation (page 85) and Sensual Touch (page 96) exercises.

Lack of time also significantly affects learning to orgasm. As we discussed earlier, most women require time to be able to orgasm. The only way to deal with this is to simply make time (page 76). There is no way to rush this. I promise you that you will look back on this time with pride and happiness.

The last major obstacle is just a lack of know-how and experience. This is very common. Fortunately, it's also very curable. All you have to do is seek information from the correct sources, practice, keep a sense of humor, and practice more.

Pre-Orgasmic to Pro-Orgasmic

As I mentioned to the men in the Orgasmic Mastery for Men chapter (page 143), some of these exercises may be most easily done with your own hands. Research has shown that women often have a much easier time learning to climax when they are in direct control, rather than having their partner direct the scene. Having the partner be in control is more likely to cause her to feel self-conscious or make her worry if her partner is getting bored. When a woman is learning to intensify her orgasms, she should be focused on her own sensations.

When women are being touched by their partners, they often censor their responses and endure unpleasant touch to protect their partner's feelings. Sometimes they pretend to feel aroused (or even pretend to orgasm) for their partner's benefit. Because of all of these factors, simply put, learning to climax is much easier done by direct self-touch. However you feel about the appropriateness of self-touch, I invite you and your partner to reread Chapter 2 and arrive at decisions that work for both of you.

Just like the Male Ejaculation Control exercise (page 153), the following exercise can be adapted for partner use.

Exercise: Claiming Your Orgasm

- ♪ Prepare a time and place where you won't be interrupted. Give yourself enough time to be able relax and take things slowly. Lock the bathroom or bedroom door, and turn off all the phones.

- ♪ Set a relaxing mood. Play some light music, light a few candles, maybe take a bath. Do whatever you need to do to feel relaxed and sensual. You may want to begin by enjoying giving yourself non-sexual touch in a modified version of the Sensual Touch exercise (page 96) from earlier in this book.

- ♪ Bring with you a bottle of personal lubricant, a vibrator, a mirror, and a timer. The lubricant is designed to help minimize chafing and make your self-exploration more enjoyable. The vibrator is to help with the stimulation. Most women need extra stimulation, and a vibrator works very well for this. If you need recommendations on a specific vibrator or lubricant, please see the chapter on sex toys and lubricants (page 195). (If you're taking a bath, water-based lubricant may wash away too quickly.) The mirror is to help you to learn about your sexual anatomy. The timer is to alert you to when you need to stop the exercise. It's much easier to let go and really concentrate on your sensations when you're not trying to keep one eye on the clock.

Step 1: Sexual Exploration

§ Apply a generous amount of lubricant to your fingers, then spread the lubricant around your genitals.

§ Using the mirror and your fingers, explore your genitals. Locate your inner and outer lips. Also locate your vaginal opening and clitoris. Your clitoris is the sensitive area at the top of where your inner lips come together, just above the urethral (urinary) opening.

§ As you explore your genitals, notice what they feel and look like. Enjoy the sensations that your touch brings, even if it's strange or unfamiliar. Notice both the sensations in your fingers and in your genitals.

§ Next, move your fingers inside your vagina. Notice what the inside of your vagina feels like on your fingers and what the pressure of your fingers feels like inside your vagina.

- With a finger or two inside your vagina, try to locate your G-spot. The G-spot is the area inside the vagina on the front/top wall (toward your belly button) between the vaginal entrance and the cervix. It may have a rough feeling and swell with prolonged stimulation. (Despite the name "spot," it's actually more of an area or zone, so don't go looking for a magic sex button.) If you can't find your G-spot, don't worry. It is sometimes difficult to discern, and you can always try to find it again later.
- When you're done exploring, think about your experience. Did it bring up positive or negative feelings? What did you like or dislike? If you had negative feelings, can you discern why?
- Depending on your experience, either go to Step 2 or stop with Step 1 for today. You may want to perform Step 1 a few times before moving on to Step 2.

Step 2: Sexual Cultivation

- Just like with Step 1, set up a quiet, relaxing environment where you won't be disturbed. Recline on pillows or in the bath.
- Start by touching, rubbing, and caressing parts of your body other than your clitoris or G-spot. Touch your body all over, feeling your legs, your stomach, and your breasts.
- When you start to be aroused, move to genital touch. Lubricate your fingers and begin to

stimulate yourself. Depending on how sensitive you are, you might be able to start stimulating your clitoris right away. If this is uncomfortable, back off and give more attention to your outer lips, then move to your inner lips. Then return to your clitoris. There is no right or wrong here, just what you like best. So pay attention to your feelings, and see what you like.

⸎ Rub, squeeze, or flick your clitoris using your fingers. See what feels best. And remember, strokes that are too intense at the beginning may not be too intense later on, when you're more aroused.

⸎ Also experiment with the vibrator. When using the vibrator, start with a light touch. Pushing the vibrator too strongly against yourself can leave you feeling numb and overstimulated. Experiment with different pressures in different places. Each spot will give you a different sensation. Some women like vibration right up on the clitoris. Others prefer a more diffuse sensation. See what you like best.

⸎ To practice stimulating your G-spot, insert fingers or the vibrator into your vagina and rub against the front wall. How does this feel? Is it pleasurable? If it doesn't do anything for you yet, move on. We'll come back to the G-spot later.

⸎ Alternate tensing and relaxing your pelvic, leg, and abdominal muscles. What does this do to your arousal? Arch your back and thrust your pelvis up and down. What effect does this have on your sensation?

- Continue stimulating yourself, following your enjoyment. Don't let the intensity of your feelings scare you. Welcome them and give in to them.

- Remember, there is no normal amount of time that it takes to achieve an orgasm. Take as long as you want, without worrying about the time.

- Also, if you don't climax the first time, don't worry. For some women, learning to experience orgasm is something that takes some time. Don't rush yourself. Just enjoy the journey. You can repeat this exercise as many times as you want.

- If at any time you do feel that you might be getting close to a peak of pleasure, don't be afraid of it, and don't stop stimulating. Keep the intensity going.

- If you do experience a spike in pleasure (i.e., an orgasm), don't stop stimulating. Keep pushing through. The intensity may become quite strong and you may almost be concerned that it could become painful. (This is why French women refer to orgasms as *le petit mort*—"the little death.") Keep stimulating for as long as you can, even after your orgasm stops. This may lead you to multiple orgasms, with each one surpassing the previous one.

- Once you're done, give yourself a few minutes to simply enjoy the feelings of resolution. Think about what you've learned and congratulate yourself on your achievement.

Kegels

Another exercise that you can do to increase the frequency and intensity of your orgasms is the Kegel. I already spoke with your husbands about this exercise in the Orgasmic Mastery for Men chapter (page 143), but these exercises are just as important for you. You may have heard about Kegels from your gynecologist, but if you haven't, now's the time to start doing them. Kegels help you maintain your vaginal tone (even after aging, pregnancy, and childbirth), which can increase both your and your husband's pleasure during sex. They help to reduce your chances of incontinence, and they strengthen your vaginal muscles, making your orgasms more intense and frequent.

During a Kegel, you will tense your pelvic floor muscles. You locate these muscles by clenching your muscles to stop the flow of urine the next time you use the bathroom. Clenching those same muscles when you're not urinating is a Kegel. Try stopping the stream of urine the next several times you use the bathroom so that you can learn which muscles you want to be tensing. However, after you have learned which muscles to focus on, switch to performing Kegels sans urine. Too much clenching mid-stream can lead to incompletely emptying your bladder.

As you perform Kegel exercises, take care not to clench anywhere but your pelvic floor. Keep your abdomen, buttocks, and upper legs relaxed. Breathe normally through the exercise.

Once you've learned how to Kegel, perform this exercise everywhere. You can do it at work, while washing dishes, while taking the trash out, while watching TV—the sky's the limit! Make a practice of consistently exercising your pelvic core, and I promise you will thank yourself. If you practice every day, you'll see definite dividends in your sex life. Your muscles won't strengthen instantly, but if you're consistent, you'll notice definite changes within a few weeks. Try the following Kegel variations, or make up your own. In whatever way you choose to Kegel, you'll reap great benefits.

Exercise: Kegel

Kegel Variation 1

- ♪ Contract the PC muscle.
- ♪ Hold while you count to ten.
- ♪ Relax the PC muscle.
- ♪ Repeat for as many repetitions as you can. Try to do at least ten reps.
- ♪ Repeat several times each day, every day.

Kegel Variation 2

- ♪ Gradually contract the PC muscle from relaxed to as tight as possible for a count of five.
- ♪ Relax the PC muscle for one count.
- ♪ Repeat.

Kegel Variation 3

- ⚘ Gradually contract the PC muscle from relaxed to as tight as possible for a count of five, then relax for one count.
- ⚘ Contract the PC muscle fast and tight for one count, then relax for one count. Do this twice.
- ⚘ Contract the PC muscle fast and tight for one count, then relax for a count of ten.
- ⚘ Tighten the PC slightly for a count of five, then a little more for another five count. Tighten it completely for another count of five.
- ⚘ Relax the PC slightly for a count of five, then a little more for another count of five. Then relax the muscle completely for another five count.

Kegels during Intercourse

When you've mastered the Kegel, begin to apply it during sex. You can use Kegels to improve your pleasure in a variety of ways. Try some of the following:

- ⚘ Alternately Kegel and relax to increase arousal during sexual stimulation.
- ⚘ Kegel rapidly when orgasm is approaching to increase the intensity of your climax.
- ⚘ Kegel around him during intercourse while he's withdrawing (or if you're controlling the thrusting, as you move off of him). This provides a pleasurable "milking" sensation for him and increased stimulation for you.

§ Kegel when you and your partner are entirely still. With your partner's penis in you, begin Kegeling in a rhythmic, rippling fashion. If you get good enough at this, you can even bring your partner to climax through your vaginal contractions alone. Known as *pompoir*, this skill takes some time to learn, but it can be very pleasurable for both of you.

Advanced Skills

So, you've practiced self-exploration and self-cultivation, and you've mastered the fine art of Kegeling. Now you're ready to learn some very advanced skills and become fully proficient at achieving orgasm—including the elusive G-spot orgasm. The G-spot is directly connected to the base of the clitoris. The clitoris you see is just the tip of the iceberg. Most of the clitoris is internal and connects directly to the G-spot. If you didn't find your G-spot during the Claiming Your Orgasm exercise (page 172), get ready to go looking again.

The debate over the existence of the G-spot seems never-ending. Some people argue that the G-spot is mere myth, while others like me claim that it's the Holy Grail of female sexuality. While definitive answers are hard to come by, I personally am convinced that there is a G-spot, or as I like to call it, the G-zone. But why take my word for it? Do your own hands-on research. I guarantee that the discovery will be fun!

Exercise: G-spot Discovery

To begin finding your G-spot, first get yourself turned on any way you'd like. (Any exercise that starts like this can't be bad, right?) You can even start looking after you've had an orgasm. Because the spongy area around the G-spot engorges during sex, it will be much easier to locate if you are already aroused. In fact, for most women, the best first step toward having a G-spot orgasm is to first have a clitoral orgasm.

By Hand

§ Get into an upright position: sitting, standing, or kneeling. It's more difficult to find the G-spot when lying down. Unsexy as it sounds, you may actually have the easiest time finding it sitting on the toilet. You might also try kneeling with your knees apart or sitting on the edge of a chair.

§ Place your palm against your vulva and slowly insert a lubricated finger inside your vagina.

§ Begin feeling around on the anterior (tummy) side of the vaginal wall.

The G-spot can be difficult to identify at first, so here are a few characteristics that you can search for during your exploration:

Some texts describe it as a bean-sized area approximately one to three inches inside your vagina. The exact size and location of the G-spot varies from woman to woman, but unless your fingers are very short, you should be able to reach it. It also helps to bear down, as this pushes the G-spot closer to the vaginal opening.

The G-spot is different in texture than the rest of the vagina. Compared to the side and back walls, the spongy G-zone is coarser in texture from the rest of the vagina. Given that you can't easily see up inside your vagina, you'll be relying on texture to guide you. Feel for this slightly bumpy or ridged area.

As you stroke the G-spot, notice how it feels. Compared to the clitoris, the G-spot can take a lot more pressure and stimulation. As you stimulate it, blood circulation to the area will increase. As the G-spot begins to be engorged, you may feel it become lumpy. Some women have larger spots (up to the size of a walnut), and some have smaller.

As the G-spot continues to expand, its texture will become even more distinctive. Because different levels of arousal will cause the G-spot to expand to different degrees, feel it at different times during your stimulation to get familiar with its contours and sensitivity. The G-spot responds to pressure, and it's much more forgiving than the clitoris.

- Once you locate your G-spot, stimulate it. Press on it firmly and pull forward using a "come hither" motion with your fingers. As the area responds to the pressure, it will swell and become hard and firm, like an erect penis.
- Many women report that even if they've emptied their bladder, G-spot stimulation gives

them an urge to urinate, so if you suddenly feel like you have to pee, that's a sign that you've found the right place.

- § Continue to stimulate through the urge to urinate. If you continue to massage the area, any awkward sensations should be replaced by a strong and distinctive feeling of sexual pleasure.
- § Relax in a comfortable position while continuing to stimulate the G-spot.
- § You may find that using your free hand to press down on your abdomen just above the pubic bone improves your sensations. Experiment to see what level of pressure works best for you.
- § As you continue your stimulation, you may feel twinges or contractions in your uterus. Continue the stimulation and you may have your first G-spot orgasm.

Don't be discouraged if you have a hard time finding your G-spot, or if stimulating it feels strange. For some, G-spot stimulation is a bit of an acquired taste, but one I highly recommend.

With a Toy

You may find that it's cumbersome or tiring to adequately stimulate your G-spot with your own hand. If so, a curved G-spot vibrator or your partner's hand can be a great help.

- § A G-spot toy should be inserted with the tip pointing up toward the top/front wall of the vagina. Work it in until the tip is pressing against your G-spot.

- Just as you experimented with pressure with your fingers, do the same with your toy. For most women, the G-spot responds to firm pressure, but see what works for you. If you're using a vibrator, the sensations will be different if you press the toy firmly against the G-spot than if you simply let it rest there. You can also use the toy by pushing beyond the G-spot and then pulling it back against the deep side of the G-spot.

- Experiment with different motions. Try using your toy as if you were trying to scratch an itch; don't push it all the way in and out of your vagina, but use short, firm strokes while applying constant pressure to the G-spot.

- As you continue to become aroused, you might graduate to a more vigorous thrusting. If you're using a vibrator, try playing with the vibrations both on and off to see which you like better.

With Your Partner

Once you've learned where your G-spot is and how to stimulate it, it's time to teach your husband. He can learn the same way that you did, by feeling around on the front wall of the vagina for a spot with a different texture.

- As he feels, guide him to the right spot. Tell him what sort of pressure you like and how you want him to move.

- You can also direct him to use his other hand on your clitoris, to push down on your abdomen, or to reinforce the power of his internal hand.
- After your husband has learned to find and stimulate your G-spot with his fingers, he can also learn to do it with a toy. However, it is important that he learns to feel with his fingers first.

As you perform this exercise, don't let performance anxiety interfere with your pleasure. Sometimes people can become so fixated on achieving a certain sexual goal (multiple orgasms, simultaneous orgasm, G-spot orgasms, etc.) that they miss out on the actual joy that can be found in a sexual encounter. Ironically, too much focus on a goal actually makes it more likely that they'll fail. Remember that sexual exploration is about the journey, not the destination.

Couples Positions for G-Spot Orgasm

Once you've experienced G-spot orgasms manually, it's time to have G-spot orgasms through intercourse. There are some specific positions that better allow the penis to repeatedly stimulate the G-spot. You're free to tailor these positions to your liking to make sure that they work for you. After all, a lot of factors go into what positions will give you optimal G-spot stimulation. These include the shape and curve of his penis, your relative sizes, and the exact location of your G-spot. So fiddle with these or pick entirely new ones. As with all G-spot orgasm techniques, it will be easier to experience a G-spot orgasm after you've been aroused by a clitoral orgasm.

THE FLOWER PRESS

The Flower Press is a variation of a man-on-top position. The woman lies on her back and brings her legs up so that her knees go over her husband's shoulders. The man inserts his penis in her vagina and kneels up, lifting her off the mattress slightly. The man grabs his partner's legs for stability while she reaches for his hips. The higher she can get her pelvis off the bed, the better. Pillows under her buttocks may help alleviate any back strain. The direction of entry should allow for some sweet, sweet G-spot stimulation.

DOGGY STYLE

Rear-entry positions like doggy style make for different angles of penetration than face-to-face positions. Unless a man's penis curves upward, entering from the rear puts the man's penis in an ideal position to rub against the anterior wall of the vagina and stimulate the G-spot. To optimally position herself for G-spot stimulation, the woman should get on her hands and knees with her head up, her back arched inward, and her knees parted a little. The more the woman elevates her back, the shallower the penetration will be, but the more fully the penis will impact the G-spot.

THE BUTTERFLY

The woman may need to do some stretching and limbering up before trying this position because it can be demanding. To perform the Butterfly, the woman lies on her back on a bed or table of appropriate height. She scoots down until her rear end is near the edge and raises her legs in the air. Her partner then penetrates her and pushes her knees toward her chest; just don't push beyond her comfort level.

If the woman curls her back and raises her hips slightly, that will help her husband's penis find her G-spot. This position is plenty intense for many people, but if you want more, the woman can take things to another level by pulling her legs closer to her torso or spreading them farther apart.

FUSION

Fusion is another position that can provide G-spot stimulation. This position can sound a little complicated, but once you get into it, it can feel absolutely magical. First, the man and woman sit on the floor facing each other with their feet outstretched and their arms on the floor beside or behind them. If you do yoga, the position is like Staff Pose, although your legs will be spread and you can recline backward a bit. The woman then moves forward and leans backward so that her legs go over the man's shoulders, while using her arms to support herself. In this position, she moves forward until her vagina has taken in the man's penis. Then, using her arms and legs, she can move back and forth on her partner's penis. This position can be difficult to maintain if either of you has joint problems; it requires strong backs, knees, and shoulders.

Female Ejaculation

Some of you may be reading this and saying, "Women can ejaculate?" Others of you may be saying, "We can, and it's awesome!" A lot has been said about female ejaculation, and there's still a lot that's unknown. Like the G-spot, some claim it's a myth. However, I can testify that it is absolutely for real. Female ejaculation is also sometimes referred to as "squirting" or "gushing."

We tend to use the word "ejaculation" to refer to the act of a man expelling semen from his penis. However, the word simply means "a sudden discharging of fluid from a duct." In female ejaculation, as in male ejaculation, fluid is forcefully expelled from the urethra.

There are two types of female sexual fluids. The first is a thick, slightly acidic substance called leukorrhea. This is the liquid that lubricates the vaginal walls to enable sex and prevent infections. The second fluid is female ejaculate. This is a sweet-smelling, clear, watery fluid produced in the Skene's glands (also known as the periurethral glands, or "female prostate"), which are one component of the G-spot. While leukorrhea varies in taste, smell, color, and consistency depending on diet, a woman's menstrual cycle, and other factors, female ejaculate remains consistently sweet and clear.

Female ejaculate is expelled out of the Skene's glands and then out the urethra (where urine comes out). In some cases, female ejaculate can travel back up the urethra and into the bladder, which is called retrograde ejaculation (this can also happen in men).

In men, orgasm and ejaculation occur almost at the same time. In women, the two can be completely separate. Orgasm is not actually necessary in order for the ejaculate to be expelled. Female ejaculation is best achieved by long arousal and constant stimulation of the G-spot. This long stimulation causes fluid to build up in the Skene's glands and contributes to the swelling of the G-spot. The amount of fluid to be ejaculated depends on a variety of factors, including hydration, the length and intensity of arousal, and how many times she has ejaculated during the session. If completely engorged and able to expel it all at once, a woman may ejaculate up to two cups, but usually it's something less.

Just because it comes through the urethra doesn't mean it's urine. Just as a man can urinate and ejaculate out of his urethra, a woman can, too. However, female ejaculate can sometimes mix with a little bit of urine, and this has led to a lot of back-and-forth regarding its exact composition.

In studies where female ejaculate has been analyzed, it has been determined that it contains glucose and an enzyme known as prostatic acid phosphatase (PAP). This enzyme is a major component in semen. In men, it comes from the prostate, and the female Skene's glands seem to be homologous to the male prostate. This enzyme is not present in urine.

Female ejaculation is not difficult to do (even an anorgasmic woman can do it), but it can be difficult to learn to *allow* oneself to do. Many women sabotage their chances for female ejaculation without even knowing it. Preventing female ejaculation is easy. All you have to do is clench your PC muscle and the fluid won't come out. Because the lead-up to female ejaculation often manifests as a feeling of fullness or of needing to urinate, many women hold back and halt their own ejaculation.

When women cannot relax and push out the ejaculate, the reason is often because of inhibitions. Women are taught not to be messy or sexually assertive. Pushing out ejaculate can feel scary, icky, or unladylike. However, it can also feel like a major sexual breakthrough. Many women find that female ejaculation allows them to feel a level of freedom and uninhibited sensuality that they never have experienced before. As the fluid builds up, the woman feels the urgency to urinate, but if she goes to the restroom prior to sex, she can be assured that what she's feeling is not urine. She'll also know that it's not urine because of what is causing the urge, and this will be confirmed after she sees what she expels.

Once a woman feels this overwhelming sensation to pee, the only obstacle is a mental one—letting go. She has to let herself relax and allow the urethral sphincter to open up and then push the fluid out. It's the exact same sensation as trying to pee. But some women just can't get over the similarities, and their minds won't let it happen.

Some women may think that they can't ejaculate because they've tried it, and it hasn't worked for them. If you want to ejaculate, I encourage you to not give up. It may just be a matter of building up enough steam and overcoming the psychological issues that inhibit you sexually. However, sometimes even the most confident of women have a hard time ejaculating, so difficulties are nothing to be concerned about and are certainly not an indicator that something is wrong. Remember, ejaculation is not synonymous with orgasm. While for some women, ejaculating can be psychologically pleasing, it's rarely as satisfying as a mind-blowing, full-bodied orgasm.

Some women who experience female ejaculation worry that they have urinated on their partners. When women ejaculate without knowing what's going on, they sometimes feel embarrassed, confused, and concerned. If this has ever happened to you, don't worry. It's completely natural, and it's a skill that a lot of women work hard to learn. If you do it naturally, you're a lucky woman.

So why should a woman learn to ejaculate? First, the release can feel tremendous and satisfying. Second, it's visually appealing. Your man will likely find the sight of it very arousing (and possibly very flattering—many men have heard whisperings of "squirting orgasms" and the sexual prowess required to bring one about). Third, it's nice to be able to match and even best him at something. (I bet he never shot out two cups!) Fourth, there may actually be some health benefits. Just as male ejaculation "cleans the pipes" and can lead to better prostate health, expelling the fluid that builds up in your female prostate may be able to help you. If nothing else, it certainly helps to wash away tension.

So, if you want to experiment with female ejaculation, try the following exercise.

Exercise: Cultivating Female Ejaculation

§   In the hours prior, be sure to drink extra water in order to maximize your hydration status.

- Use the bathroom and empty your bladder. This will help you to be at ease regarding feelings of fullness or of needing to urinate.
- Lay a towel down on the bed (or wherever you have decided to do this exercise).
- Next, stimulate yourself sexually (or have your partner stimulate you). After significantly prolonged arousal (and possibly clitoral orgasm), begin G-spot stimulation.
- Take a very long time to stimulate your G-spot. The longer and more pressure you apply to your G-spot, the better.
- Once you start to feel that sensation to urinate, keep stimulating until you feel like you're going to burst. If you try to ejaculate too soon, you may not have enough pressure to make it happen, so just keep rubbing until you can't take it anymore.
- When you are at your limit, you'll need to remove everything (fingers, penis, toy) from your vagina. As you do, instead of clenching down like a Kegel, do the opposite and *bear down* as though you are trying to push urine out.
- If you expel liquid, congratulations! If you still feel the urge and pressure, you can keep stimulating your G-spot and keep ejaculating over and over until you're empty or tuckered out.
- If you can't expel it or if you only ejaculate a little, that's fine. The fluid in there will reabsorb into your body over time. For many women,

their first ejaculations are small. However, with time and more practice, they often begin to produce larger and larger quantities of female ejaculate.

Nipple Orgasms

For most people, the nipples are the second most erogenous zone. The nipples are packed with nerve endings—in both women and men—making them especially sensitive to touch. In some cases, this pleasure can lead to orgasm, but it varies quite a bit from one person to the next.

In women, the sensitivity of the nipples and breasts changes with the menstrual cycle. There is often less sensitivity during the first two weeks of the cycle, heightened sensitivity during ovulation, and then lessened sensitivity again during menstruation. And size doesn't matter to Mother Nature: women of all breast sizes can have a pleasurable reaction. In fact, some say that smaller breasts may actually be more sensitive because the same number of nerve endings are condensed into a smaller area.

Try caressing, kissing, licking, sucking, massaging, or nibbling the nipples and breasts. You can also use your tongue to trace circles around or flick the nipples. Start slowly and gently, focusing on the breast as a whole, then gradually increase pressure and nipple intensity. Figure out what feels best for you and your partner.

Keep in mind that different people like different things. Some women really enjoy lots of nipple stimulation. Some find it boring or painful. And others respond best when close to orgasm. Talk with your partner to figure out what's going to work for both of you. Even if you or your partner can't orgasm this way, it doesn't mean you can't incorporate what you've learned here in your repertoire of lovemaking skills.

Chapter 14

Toys and Lubes

Vibrations can bring on an orgasm just as well as, if not better than, a thrusting penis. Some take issue with the artificial nature of vibrators. Here's my take on it: Look at the fruits of it—whether it's interfering with your relationship intimacy or enhancing your intimacy. Using a large, lifelike, rubberized penis may be threatening to your husband, whereas a Hitachi Magic Wand may not be.

We use a whole host of modern enhancements to make our lives better: medicines, cars, phones, power tools, etc. So it's not much of a leap to allow us to use power tools to bring us pleasure. If we can use power tools to make assembling a bed easier, then why not use another set of power tools to enjoy activities in said bed?

There are so many sex toys out there, and between the time I write this and you read it, hundreds more will have hit the market. Some basic categories of toys are: dildos, vibrators, anal toys, artificial vaginas, and discipline toys. Most toys are for women because, until recently, it's been technically challenging to create something that compares to a vagina or a hand.

Sex Toy Materials Chart

	Non-Porous	Useable with silicone lube	Boilable	Phthalate free	Cost
Silicone	Yes	Yes*	Yes	Yes	$$$
Thermo-Plastic Elastomer (TPE/TPR)	No	Yes	No	Yes	$$
Jelly (PVC + Rubber)	No	No	No	No	$
Latex	No	No	No	No	$
CyberSkin (Latex + Silicone)	No	No	No	No	$$
Glass/Pyrex	Yes	Yes	Yes	Yes	$$$
Metal	Yes	Yes	Yes	Yes	$$$
Ceramic	Yes	Yes	Yes	Yes	$$$
Hard Plastic	Yes	Yes	No	Yes	$$
Acrylic	Yes	Yes	No	Yes	$$
Leather	No	No	No	Yes	$$

100% pure silicone toys can be used with 100% pure silicone lube, but not all claims of purity are accurate.

Retains heat	Carries vibration well	Soft	No smell or taste	Hypo-allergenic
Yes	Yes	Somewhat	Yes	Yes
No	Yes	Yes	No	Somewhat
No	No	Very soft	No	No
No	No	Yes	No	No
Somewhat	No	Yes	No	No
Yes	Yes	No	Yes	Yes
Yes	Yes	No	Yes	Yes
Yes	Yes	No	Yes	Yes
Yes	Yes	No	Yes	Yes
Yes	Yes	No	Yes	Yes
Yes	Somewhat	Somewhat	No	No

$ - *Less expensive than the average toy.*

$$ - *Cost of toys of this material is middle-of-the-road.*

$$$ - *More expensive than the average toy.*

A Note on Phthalates

When you are shopping for sex toys, you may see the following message: "Phthalate free." What the heck is a phthalate? Phthalates (pronounced "thal'-ates") are substances added to plastics to increase their flexibility, transparency, durability, and longevity. However, because these substances are not covalently bonded to the plastic, they easily leach out. Phthalates may contribute to health problems such as birth defects, low birth weight, breast cancer, increased insulin resistance, thyroid problems, endometriosis, precocious puberty, and more.

Lubes

I'm glad you didn't skip over this section. You'd be surprised how many people I've helped by simply handing them a bottle of silicone lube. I was honestly surprised by how many women have what I consider to be an odd objection to using lube. Some seem to see it as a sign of failure that they need to use lube—they assume that they should just naturally lubricate enough on their own. Do these same people have an objection to using body wash and deodorant? Lube is fabulous! Use it!

Also, recognize that not all lubes are created equal. I'd been married for at least ten years before I learned of anything other than just water-based lube. I am very biased now. Until you've used a pure silicone lube, I don't want to hear about your other favorites.

SALIVA

The first and most ubiquitous lubrication is saliva. Your body makes it, so you always have it with you, and unless you're sick, it's fairly safe to use. There's debate about whether it contributes to yeast infections, but it's no worse than most water-based lubes. Compared to some other options, saliva isn't very slippery, so it is not ideal for prolonged use. However, if a woman produces a lot of natural lubricant by herself, using a bit of saliva to "prime the pump" could be helpful. But guys, please do not just spit down there. That is so not sexy. Just don't.

WATER-BASED LUBRICANTS

You can buy cheap water-based lubricants at almost any grocery store. You're probably familiar with the traditional K-Y Jelly with which newlyweds start most often, and if they never graduate to anything else, they may start wondering what's so great about lube. Water-based lube does have some benefits: it washes off easily, does not irritate the skin, and is condom- and toy-safe. The negatives are that, because of water evaporation and absorption, it dries out and becomes tacky. So just when you need it to be slick, it turns into glue. Although you can refresh it with a few drops of water or saliva, this lubricant is not the best for long-lasting play.

Type of Lube	Brands	Recommendations
Silicone	Pjur	Silicone lubes are my favorite. I love the fact that silicone doesn't get "tacky," doesn't have a taste, makes my skin soft, and can be used as a massage oil.
Water-based	Liquid Silk Wet Original	Unless using toys or on a budget, there is very little advantage to water-based lubricants over silicone.
Warming	K-Y Touch Massage	Can be fun for a massage only. Silicone lube works better as a lube and as a body massage.
Mousse	Intimate Options from Replens	Fun to try, but for the money there are much better products on the market.
Scented	K-Y Yours + Mine	Fun to try as a change of pace, but not an everyday lubricant. Try it out in a sensitive area before the big night so you'll know if you like the sensation first!
Flavored	Wet Brand Flavored	A fun novelty lubricant, but may not be best for everyday use. Great for learning to give blow jobs.
Fertility	Pre-Seed, ConceivEase, Yes Baby, Conceive Plus, and Zestica.	If you're trying to get pregnant, use this or use no lube at all. Don't use saliva either, as the acidity destroys sperm.

Advantages	Disadvantages
Great for massage and dry skin. Doesn't get sticky like water-based lube. Longest-lasting lube. Doesn't dry out. Doesn't break down in water, so it can be used in hot tubs, showers, etc. No taste or odor. Latex-friendly. Doesn't react with skin. Doesn't get absorbed into the skin or tissues. Doesn't stain.	Since it is a silicone, it will bond with some toys and ruin them. You must either use a condom over soft toys or wash them off immediately after use.
Great for vaginal sex. Doesn't stain. Safe for condoms and all toys.	Becomes tacky and sticky as it dries. Needs to be reapplied frequently. Tastes gross.
Can be used as a body massage and as a lube. Has a warming action. Can be used with a condom. Claims to be fragrance-free and non-staining.	Warming action may be irritating to the vaginal mucus membrane, which can be distracting during intercourse. May or may not have the same effect for the penis. Tastes awful and has a strange smell.
Not messy. Won't drip or run. Easy to clean up. Water-based, so you can use it with all sex toys and condoms. Doesn't stain.	Like all water-based lubes, can become sticky. Doesn't last as long as other lubes.
Great for vaginal sex. Smells good. Creates new sensations when mixed. Fun as a novelty.	If you have sensitive skin, this isn't for you. The more the lubes mix, the more stimulating (and potentially irritating) they can become.
Sugar-free, colorless, non-staining, and safe with latex and silicone toys. They smell good and should taste good. Great for oral sex.	Many flavored lubes have an aftertaste. Because they are water-based, they become tacky and need to be reapplied.
Unlike every other kind of lube (including saliva), these do not interfere with sperm function. If you're trying to get pregnant, fertility lubes are really the only choice.	Most brands contain methylparaben and propylparaben, preservatives, which irritate some people.

OIL-BASED LUBRICANTS

There are a few commercial oil-based lubricants out there, but it's more common for couples to use pure olive oil and coconut oil as lubricants. While these all-natural lubes make for good massage oils, they may break condoms, have an odor, and stain fabric.

SILICONE LUBRICANTS

My personal favorite is pure silicone lube. It's not absorbed by the body, so it won't get sticky. It provides a smooth, slippery feeling unlike any other sort of lubrication. It's odorless and tasteless. But like oil-based lube, silicone may not be compatible with all condoms and toys. If silicone lube is left in contact with jelly or rubbery sex toys, it can ruin them. After play, wash your toys off with soapy water. Even though pure silicone lube is considerably more expensive than water-based lube, a few drops go a long way. I suggest keeping a cruet of lube on your nightstand.

FERTILITY LUBRICANTS

Many lubricants hinder conception for one reason or another. Fertility lubricants (also known as "sperm-friendly lubricants") remove these obstacles to conception. They are specially developed to avoid damaging sperm. If you are trying to conceive, make sure that you are using a fertility lubricant, because any other form of lubrication (including saliva) can hinder conception.

SPECIALTY LUBRICANTS

There are also a number of specialty lubricants that can be fun as an occasional novelty. These include warming lubricants, tingling lubricants, and flavored lubricants. Be cautious that flavored lubes don't have sugar. You don't want to put anything in your vagina that organisms can survive on. Glycerin is a common additive in lubes; whether additives help or hurt is dependent on the individual.

Fun with Lubes

Lubricant will contribute to your sex life by making the engagement more pleasurable. Here are a few tips for use when adding lubes to your play:

- † Warm up your lube before applying it by submerging the bottle in warm water. You can also use an oil warmer like the kind used by massage therapists.
- † Put the lube on your hands first, then transfer the lube to the genitals. This warms it to body temperature and avoids shocking your partner.
- † Maybe you want to shock your partner—pour it all over from a little ways up.

With any lube, the precise characteristics can vary greatly based on brand. You may need to experiment with different brands to find what works best for you.

Chapter 15

Sexual Exploration and Communication

I was once asked to be interviewed for a TV news piece to offer my insights on kinky sex and how it relates to violence toward women. The news piece was to be a follow-up on the popularity of the book *Fifty Shades of Grey*. The reporter asked me if I could help her find some BDSM[7] practitioners she could interview along with myself. A client couple agreed to be interviewed in my office, and a friend of mine who owns a sex toy shop was also featured in the story.

---

7 Bondage, Domination, Submission, and Masochism are a few of the sexual play styles that are often included in the broad rubric of "kink."

When I saw the final piece air on TV, I had to laugh. The reporter clearly had a specific agenda she wanted to promote, regardless of what any of us actually said. Our statements were taken out of context, twisted to fit her angle, and edited together to convey the exact opposite of what we had intended.

In addition to teaching me a valuable lesson about the media, this experience led me to reflect on something that I've taught couples for a long time: clear and honest communication is an absolute necessity when it comes to adventuresome sex.

I am often asked how I can be a faithful Latter-day Saint Christian and not be opposed to kink. First of all, it's my job to have some awareness and understanding of everything in the world of sexology. Without that understanding, I might not be able to help couples that approach sexuality from a non-traditional angle. The way I see it, my job and calling is to educate and assist people, not to make judgments on their sexual interests or activities. My clients make the moral choices regarding what elements they want in their sex lives; I help them navigate these choices and find joy and satisfaction within the frameworks they create.

Of course, gaining an understanding of various sex acts doesn't necessarily mean that I personally embrace them all. (If I personally practiced everything I've been exposed to in sexology, I would be one tired and sore girl!) But in my research and my practice, I've seen more than you can imagine, and I will share my knowledge when it's appropriate.

Second, there are many levels of this kind of sexual power play. For example, think about the power balance in your own sex life. Is it always 50/50? Most definitely not. It's nearly impossible to have your sexual exchange be perfectly balanced at every moment—you both can't be on top at the same time. Of course, you can strive for a 50/50 average over an evening or over a couple of sessions, and I find that couples are happiest when they do so. But when you engage in an unbalanced exchange, even momentarily, you are then practicing a mild form of domination and submission.

While your imbalances may be unintended and shifting, those who intentionally engage in BDSM desire this imbalance, prepare for it, acknowledge it, and improve upon it. The best BDSM practitioners manage the give-and-take of sex in a conscious and emotionally healthy way that follows predefined boundaries and rules.

I wish to state plainly here that I am not one who supports what is traditionally referred to as masochism. Though I recognize that some people experience pain as pleasure, and may derive sexual pleasure from this kind of encounter, I do not personally encourage the uninitiated use of this type of play, especially for an inexperienced couple, as it can lead to serious emotional and physical harm.

I personally believe that whether or not couples plan on formally incorporating BDSM practices in their relationship, they need to acknowledge and manage the imbalances that are inherent in sex. If we ignore these imbalances, we perpetuate ignorance of our roles in our relationship. This willful disregard can lead to frustration and diminished intimacy. This is the main reason that I teach a workshop titled "BDSM and Kink"—I want couples to learn to openly communicate about the imbalances inherent in sex.

In some kink relationships, one partner is always the dominant (Dom) and the other is always the submissive

(Sub). However, for other couples, partners switch between roles. People who alternate between roles of dominance and submission are, appropriately enough, called "switches."

I believe that couples who are "switches" are happiest, even if they temporarily agree that one will be a firm Dom while the other is a willing Sub. Being switches allows you to seek equality in your marriage and to experience different types of intimacy. It's one sort of intimacy to be completely on equal footing with your spouse, another to completely surrender yourself to your partner's control, and still another to realize that they have completely surrendered themselves to you.

Another benefit of BDSM is the need for trust. Kinky sex can be a very vulnerable experience, both physically and emotionally, and the act of completely letting go can be a big intimacy boost. But it does require trust. For some couples, the trust that they learn and demonstrate during kinky sex spills into other aspects of the relationship, bringing both strength and intimacy to the whole marriage.

Do I need to state the obvious that no one should *ever* force their partner to participate in BDSM activities? They are and must be strictly consensual. If not, it's not kink—it's rape.

While I'm not encouraging you to practice BDSM sex play, I do want you to see that this type of advanced sexual engagement does have its own useful set of rules.

The Five Principles

For practitioners of BDSM, there are five basic principles that must be followed in order to ensure the safety and satisfaction of both partners.

CONSENT

Consent separates kink from abuse. Securing consent from a partner is a necessity, even if you've been married for years. Never assume anything. When you ask for consent, be explicit and direct: "I need to know you've agreed to this before we begin." This is not the time for hinting or indirection. Both parties need to know exactly what's involved and that both agree to the activity.

Giving consent establishes that you're both ready, willing, and able to proceed, that you've discussed what's likely to happen, shared any concerns, and talked about your limits. When you give consent, you agree to play, to communicate during the scene, and to stop if needed.

NEGOTIATION

An honest negotiation about what you both expect from the interaction is critically important, as this allows both partners to talk about their needs, wants, limits, fantasies, and fears before play. Before you begin, identify what role(s) you will take: dominant/submissive,[8] top/bottom, switch, etc. Propose some possible scenarios and decide if you are interested in them. For each one, you can decide whether you want to give or receive (or both).

Make a "Yes, No, Maybe" list of all the possible sexual interests/kinks that either of you can imagine. I could sug-

---

8   The "dominant" or "Dom" controls the scene. The "submissive" or "Sub" is the one being controlled. The "Top" is the one doing the action. The "Bottom" is receiving the action. The Dom and Top may be the same person, but a Dom can also be a Bottom if the Dom is directing the Sub to do something to him/her.

gest a list, but I don't want to put anything in your minds that you don't want there. (Use your imagination to come up with a list, or use the Internet.) Put in the "yes" column all the things you'd like to do, all the things you won't do in the "no" column, and in the "maybe" column those activities that fall in between.

Discuss the things you've placed in the "maybe" column. Why are they there? Under what circumstances would you be willing to try them? It's fine for you to have something in the "no" column while your partner has the same activity in the "yes" or "maybe" column. If something is firmly in either of your "no" columns, then take it off the table for now.

I would hope that you'd already know this about each other, but if either of you has any aversions or phobias, you should reveal them now. You don't want to unexpectedly unmask something during playtime.

SAFETY AND SAFEWORDS

A safeword is a word or phrase that you and your partner choose as a sort of safety net. If you don't like something that's happening and you want the scene to stop right away, simply say your safeword. It is of utmost importance that the safeword always be obeyed; it is sacred. Disregarding or ignoring it is an inexcusable breach of trust.

Words like "stop," "no," or "please don't" are not ideal safewords because they may be part of the dialogue of a scene where the bottom wants to resist or be forced to do something. Similarly, long or difficult-to-remember words or phrases are not good choices (so "antidisestablishmentarianism" and "honorificabilitudinitatibus" are out). You want to pick a word that is easy to remember and say, but that is unlikely to come up during the scene. Mine is "Diet Coke." But I've never had to use it.

If you're a couple who knows each other well and can read body language, then each of you should be able to recognize when you're reaching each other's limits. If you find that you're using your safeword a lot, then maybe you're not really reading each other well or you're too willing to cross established boundaries.

COMMUNICATION

Communication is a huge part of kink, and it is one of the reasons that I'm not as opposed to it as some would think I should be. Communication is critical to preparation for BDSM. The people who have the best experiences are the ones who know how to clearly state what they want. BDSM practitioners often prepare for hours before they play. They negotiate, ask questions of each other, and reveal their own feelings, fears, and desires.

Verbal communication can also continue into the scene itself, and it probably should, at least while you are still feeling your way into things. Honest feedback can help to make things more pleasant, even if it breaks the mood a little. This sort of communication lays the groundwork for future play, and it's much better than simply enduring something that you truly dislike.

In any situation, eye contact and nonverbal communication are critical. You should each be able to read the other's body language and facial expressions and use these to decide whether something should continue, ratchet up, or wind down.

I'm going to let you in on a little secret: being the Dom doesn't mean that you're in total control. Because you're a caring person, the Sub's desires should equally control the play. A good Dom must be aware of the Sub's needs and choreograph the scene to meet them. Doms who act selfishly and only gratify their own desires won't be allowed to stay in that role for long.

AFTERCARE

Kinky sex play can bring up a wide range of unexpected emotions. No matter which role you play in a session, you have the responsibility to care for the physical and emotional well-being of your partner. After you've addressed basic needs like cleaning up and drinking some water, it's time to attend to each other's emotions.

Even if you're not ready to talk about all of your feelings, it's important for you two to stay together and process your most pressing feelings right away. Be ready to listen, validate, cuddle, and offer comfort. You always want to ensure that your spouse knows that you love and care about them, regardless of what roles you may have played during a scene. It's also a good idea to discuss things a couple of days later to see if any new feelings have come up, especially before you schedule another play date.

Whether or not you believe in, support, or practice BDSM or kinky sex, these five principles can be incorporated into most sexual relationships, as they encourage communication, compromise, and understanding the desires of your partner. If you decide to explore these avenues of sexual play, please do so carefully; otherwise, you can seriously damage your relationship. If kink is not for you, take the lessons on communication included in this chapter to heart anyways, and use them in whatever sexual avenues you choose to explore together.

Chapter 16

Continuing Your Education

You've almost made it to the end of this book, and I hope that it's been a productive experience. Hopefully you've learned techniques and skills that have improved your relationship and sex life. Hopefully you've even internalized some ideas that affect the way you think about and approach sex.

Where will you go from here? Just keep learning as a couple and enjoy the never-ending journey of sexual growth. Make sexual experimentation a priority, and use your imagination. If you focus on your sensations, actively search for new ways to please your partner and yourself, and really treat your sex life as something beautiful and important, you'll find that you are constantly finding ways to improve your sexual relationship.

Some desire more education and information than can be found in this book or through their own imagination. Here are a few avenues for furthering your sexual education.

First, you can personally meet with a sexologist. Often, couples wait to visit with a counselor as a last-ditch effort to save a relationship, but visiting with a professional can also be useful when you're just wanting to add a little spice to the relationship. Think of it as taking your car in for a regular tune-up, rather than just waiting for the "Check Engine" light to come on.

You can also attend classes or workshops. I teach a number of seminars that cover topics like oral sex, anal sex, BDSM and kink, and advanced orgasm techniques. I always love it when my readers show up to my seminars, and if you're ever in an area where I'm teaching a workshop, I would love to meet you. There are also others who teach about sexuality, and many of them have something worthwhile to teach you. You might learn something from the sales person at your local sex toy store. Many toy stores host classes on sexuality, and even if they don't, there's a decent chance that they will know of any classes in the area.

Finally, you can find limitless resources online. Deciding to look for information on the web has its risks and benefits. There's no restriction on the range of what you'll find, and once you learn something, you can't unlearn it. If one spouse is searching while the other one isn't, the interest gap can cause a split in the relationship. Be cautious. It's difficult to know exactly what effect any given piece of educational material will have on a couple.

In some cases, something may even be helpful and educational at first, but open the door to more explicit and harmful materials later. In these cases, a couple may later wish that they'd never opened that first door. For this reason, I suggest that all couples who choose to use more sexually explicit materials ease into things. This reduces both the chances of being shocked and the chances that you'll experience unnecessary guilt (page 31). It all comes down to what works best for your marriage. Continue to discuss the instructive materials that you use.

Conclusion

One of the beautiful things about married sex is that because you are in a committed, long-term relationship, you have the time to get to know how to perfectly dance with your partner. There's really no limit to how good you can get at pleasuring your lover. You are learning to be a virtuoso at pleasing them, and there's no reason why every year you can't have better sex than the year before. Because the two of you are in a committed relationship, you have the rare opportunity to spend the rest of your lives learning the ins and outs of each other's bodies and souls.

Of course, there are a lot of people who have been playing the same instrument for years, but have never become a virtuoso. One of the large differences is practice. Even though you have finished this book, I hope you haven't finished practicing your intimate skills. Most of all, though, I hope that you and your mate always find satisfaction, joy, and love in your encounters with each other.

Now get out there and have some fun together!

Index